# PILGRIMAGE
# REVEALED

## A DEVOTIONAL STUDY OF FIRST PETER

ALLEN SATTERLEE

CREST
BOOKS

Crest Books
The Salvation Army National Headquarters
615 Slaters Lane
Alexandria, VA 22313
Phone: 703-684-5523

Lt. Colonel Tim Foley, *National Secretary for Program
& Editor-in-Chief*
Alexanderia Saurman, *Editorial Assistant*
Joshua Morales, *Lead Graphic Designer*

Available in print from crestbooks.com.

ISBN: 978-1-946709-88-2

# CONTENTS

# INTRODUCTION

Have you ever wondered what it would have been like to meet Jesus during His earthly ministry? What was it like to walk along the way and talk with Him, knowing that only a sliver of what He said is recorded in our Gospels? What of living through the revolution that came when Christ rose from the grave? Those who refused to believe were confronted with an unimaginable task of denying the new reality. Those who believed lived in the euphoria of a victory so complete as to have no equal anywhere else in time or eternity. And then to see the church take shape, the gospel powerfully preached and people of all races and backgrounds bending their knee in submission to the King of kings and the Lord of lords! Peter experienced all of that. No one showed a more radical change than did this erstwhile fisherman of Galilee.

Forever different, Peter's days were crowded with victories, setbacks, glory and disappointment. His little book of First Peter represents some of his last words to the believers who must take up the battle as he faced his fate as a martyr. When we read First Peter, we are in the mind and heart of this disciple who, with John, experienced and unequalled intimacy with the Savior during His earthly ministry. In his mind he had turned over again and again the things Jesus said and did. He understood what it all meant as he could not when Jesus stood within touching distance of him. The Holy Spirit now illumined him, quickening his spirit and guiding him as he relived and continued to live his adventure in Christ. And as you read this book, you will share what God shared with him. It is not a mystery. It is there before you in black and white (or bytes).

There is almost universal agreement that these are, indeed, the words of Peter. Although some have tried to argue otherwise, their arguments are more from efforts to disprove Peter's authorship than any clear evidence of some other author. Since the early Church fathers, Peter has been overwhelmingly said to be the author of the epistle.

The likely place where he wrote it was Rome, at a

time when his death appeared imminent. It is dated some time before 70 A.D. when Titus destroyed the Temple in Jerusalem. If it had already been destroyed, no doubt Peter would have made mention of it, particularly when he spoke of the body of believers forming the new Temple (1 Peter 2:5-9).

There are several prominent themes. He took great pains to warn believers of persecution, of its necessity, its purifying influence and how it was unavoidable, particularly in this time, as an unavoidable cost of discipleship. Coupled with that was his desire to lift their eyes to see the long view of persecution, the coming glory of Christ's kingdom and their place in it. In Peter's eyes these are inextricably connected. Woven throughout are the ideas of Christian hope, the church as the new expression of God's people and practical matters in the daily life of the church.

When reading the book, it is important to remember that it was meant to be read aloud in the congregation. This was partially necessary because many of the early converts could not read but also it allowed believers to stop along the way, discuss and digest what Peter was saying to them. We are tremendously enriched by this short letter and only regret that Peter did not write more of them.

Finally, I would like to thank those who helped me with this book. Major Frank Duracher, a deeply valued friend and highly valued colleague, reviewed and assisted in making helpful changes to the manuscript. The Salvation Army National Headquarters Publications staff led by Lt. Colonel Tim Foley, went above and beyond to get this book ready for publication. I am deeply grateful.

# 1
# TO THE EXILES

*Peter, an apostle of Jesus Christ,*
*To God's elect, exiles scattered throughout the*
*provinces of Pontus, Galatia, Cappadocia, Asia*
*and Bithynia, who have been chosen according*
*to the foreknowledge of God the Father, through*
*the sanctifying work of the Spirit, to be obedient*
*to Jesus Christ and sprinkled with His blood:*
*Grace and peace be yours in abundance.*
1 Peter 1:1-2

When meteorologists see weather that is likely
to spawn tornadoes, they send out warnings using
every practical means so that people can take proper
precautions. If an actual tornado forms nearby, any

hope of fleeing its path is likely useless, so instructions go out to find shelter as quickly as possible until the storm has passed. Even with these efforts, sometimes there is injury, loss of life and property. But if that happens it will not be for lack of effort to warn potential victims.

Peter could see the storm clouds on the horizon. He was also fully aware that Christians were already being increasingly alienated from those around them. The letter we are reading accomplishes a number of purposes. Primarily, Peter reminded them of what they would have to go through as well as notifying them of the difficulty that lay ahead.

After identifying himself using the Greek form of the name Jesus had given him (Peter), he reminded them that he was an apostle, literally "sent one," and that in that office he had something important to share. He noted immediately their status: exiles.

Some have thought that means that these were Christians who had fled Nero's persecution, a brief but particularly violent time when believers were hunted and suffered gruesome, violent deaths. No doubt they were in Peter's mind. But more likely he was addressing his readers as exiles because in their hometowns, in the countries of their citizenship, by following Christ they had become internal exiles, no longer in harmony with the world in which they lived.

The formation of a new people of God was an important theme that Peter wove throughout the epistle. They were exiles, stranger, wanderers, chosen, elect, living stones, the people of God. It hardly mattered what they were before. It was what they were now, what they were becoming and where they were heading. They were on a pilgrimage while staying in place, citizens of a new kingdom while coping with the empire that increasingly regarded them as a threat, a pestilence, an object for extermination.

The area where the letter was sent is in what is now northern Turkey and followed a common trade route. Scholars are divided as to whether or not Peter had himself been to this area, nor do we have any record of Paul having been there. It is likely that some forgotten evangelists carried the gospel message and established the churches. In whatever way it happened, they were important enough to gain Peter's notice.

Peter spoke of the exiles as being God's "elect." Theologically, the Calvinist idea of election means that God choses who will and will not be saved regardless of a person's free will. The message of the New Testament is something quite different. When a person receives the gift of salvation by resigning his or her will to the Lord, seeking His forgiveness and being born again, that person becomes one of the elect. It means that in being born again, there is more than forgiveness of sin or even entry into heaven. It means that, as Witherington says, "God has a destiny for them and a way of living for Christians."[1]

Peter gave us a beautiful picture of the Trinity at work. The Father foreknew, the Holy Spirit sanctified, and the Son saved us through the sprinkling of His blood. In the beauty of the mystery that is the Trinity, the great Three-in-One is at work in every moment, initiated at the moment a person receives Christ as Savior.

Their situation had not come as a surprise to God. Peter said it was according to God's foreknowledge. The concept of God's foreknowledge has been something that theologians and biblical scholars have wrestled with for centuries. The Bible is not specific in what foreknowledge encompasses or how it all works in every detail. Suffice it to say, it is a fact and it means that God has never lost sight of us, never been surprised by the things that have surprised us, never been baffled by the things that stupefy us. Where we are, the circumstances of our lives, our gifts, talents, liabilities and shortcomings are not only fully known to God but are the tools for Him to use us and work in us where we are in this moment and where we find ourselves tomorrow. This is not to say that God ordains sin but that He knows what to do with the broken pieces.

Sanctification literally means "set apart" and, in this sense, means set apart for God's service. The Holy Spirit prepares us for service by His work of purifying and filling us so that we can be used by God. Sin has done terrible damage to who and what God meant for us to be, but the Holy Spirit moves in and in His wonderful way repairs and prepares us. We are not left to ourselves to fix what is wrong. We bring all of what we are and let the Holy Spirit in His work of sanctification make us what we could not possibly ever be without Him.

The reference to Jesus speaks of our obedience made possible because we "are sprinkled with His blood." The reference hearkens back to Exodus 24:5-8. When Moses was dedicating the altar, he took half of the sacrificial blood and sprinkled the altar. With the other half, he sprinkled the people, signifying their redemption. Obviously, only a small portion of the Israelites were literally sprinkled, but in the salvation we have in Christ every believer is sprinkled with the redeeming blood of the Lamb.

## DISCUSSION QUESTIONS

1. In what ways are believers exiles in today's world?

2. The author quotes Dr. Witherington, who says that being one of God's elect means He has a destiny for them. How does that make you view your life?

3. In what ways can the Holy Spirit help to fix what is wrong in us? What might He not change?

# 2
# LIVING HOPE

*Praise be to the God and Father of our Lord
Jesus Christ! In His great mercy He has given
us new birth into a living hope through the
resurrection of Jesus Christ from the dead,
and into an inheritance that can never perish,
spoil or fade. This inheritance is kept in heaven
for you, who through faith are shielded by
God's power until the coming of the salvation
that is ready to be revealed in the last time.*
1 Peter 1:3-5

Eugene Lang was a self-made multi-millionaire
known for his wise investments and frugal living.
Invited back for a graduation speech to PS 121,

his old elementary school, his life instead took a turn that eventually would give hope to 16,000 students. He intended to give them a pep talk about working hard but, as he recalled, "I looked out at that audience of almost entirely black and Hispanic students…I began telling them about Martin Luther King's 'I Have a Dream' speech, and that everyone should have a dream. Then I decided to tell them I'd give a scholarship to every member of the class admitted to a four-year college." There was a gasp. It was followed by him being mobbed by the students and teachers. The principal told him he would only have to honor the promise to one or two students. Instead, with this hope in hand, over half went on to college.[2]

To temper his message of persecution, throughout this epistle Peter reminded believers that there was much more than what was happening in the moment. He started with his doxology of praise to God and for what He has done.

The first gift mentioned was mercy. Those most conscious of what they have been, what they might have become or where their temptations even now might lead them rejoice that God greeted them with mercy. Ours is a miserable, hopeless condition without Christ. We need nothing less than His mercy.

What did His mercy provide? Peter says, "a new birth into a living hope." The old life could not be patched, reconditioned, or recycled. We needed nothing less than a total new life as furnished through the gift of salvation. As Witherington has noted, "We can no more cause ourselves to be born again than we can cause ourselves to be born the first time."[3]

The new birth spawns our hope. With the persecution that was already happening and the growing adversity that the future was to bring, they had to be grounded in hope. By citing the resurrection of Christ, Peter was reminding them that the bleakest moment in human history was swallowed up in the victory of Easter morning. Our hope is grounded in the energy of death dying, in the futility of a useless stone trying to hold back the resurrected Christ.

God has also provided "an inheritance that can never perish, spoil or fade." Already, refugee Christians had lost claim to their ancestral homes and land, had watched their life's savings confiscated or, if they managed to spirit any away, prey to thieves that plagued their flight. Many who had not yet experienced this loss nevertheless felt its threat looming, and with it, intruding thoughts and worries of how they might cope.

It was common for wealth to be held in vaults in the largest temple in ancient cities with the hope that the god would protect it. Even this was not secure as fire could consume the building, or an invading army loot the temple. Vermin could eat away at precious garments or rust could melt objects away.

Peter told them that their inheritance was something better. As the Church Father Bede said, "Our inheritance is imperishable because it is a heavenly life which neither age nor illness nor death nor any plague can touch. It is undefiled because no unclean person can enter into it. It is unfading, because the heavenly blessings are such that even after long enjoyment of them the blessed never grow tired, whereas those who live in earthly luxury eventually have their fill of it and turn away from it."[4]

To Jewish listeners, the idea of an inheritance would remind them of the guarantee made to the children of Israel regarding the Promised Land. Even to the present the land of Israel represents a hope for a settled, secure and peaceful existence. Unfortunately, the land of Israel has been anything but that. The inheritance provided by Christ will supply the heart desire that parcels of land or riches stored away can never satisfy.

This inheritance is not only something for the present day but will go on until Christ comes to establish His reign on earth in total victory. The declaration of hope was in sharpest contrast to the prevailing view of the day. As Jobes notes, "In Greek thought, the despair of this life is followed only by the unending night of death. Catullus writes that though the sun can set and rise again, once our brief light sets there is but one unending night to be slept through." She further notes, "Christian hope is everlasting because Christ, the ground of hope, is everlasting."[5]

The hope we have is not some wistful, dreamy notion that someday, somehow everything will magically get better. It is a full gripped, confident assurance based on the certainty that the God who stood above the nothingness that preceded creation and spoke it into being will deliver on His promise to us.

## DISCUSSION QUESTIONS

1. Why do some people lose hope?

2. Given that these believers faced the loss of all they had, how could Peter's words keep them from despair?

3. Describe what you think your inheritance will look when Christ returns to set up His kingdom on earth. What will your life be like and how will your inheritance play into it?

# 3

# GREATER THAN GOLD

*In all this you greatly rejoice, though now for a little while you may have had to suffer grief in all kinds of trials. These have come so that the proven genuineness of your faith—of greater worth than gold, which perishes even though refined by fire—may result in praise, glory and honor when Jesus Christ is revealed. Though you have not seen Him, you love Him; and even though you do not see Him now, you believe in Him and are filled with an inexpressible and glorious joy, for you are receiving the end result of your faith, the salvation of your souls.*
1 Peter 1:6-9

*The International Standard Bible Encyclopedia* describes the ancient method used to process gold:

> "The ore was first crushed to the size of lentils and then ground to powder in a hand mill made of granite slabs. This powder was spread upon a slightly inclined stone table and water was poured over it to wash away the earthy materials. The comparatively heavy gold particles were then gathered from the table, dried, and melted in a closed crucible with lead, salt and bran, and kept in a molten condition for 5 days, at the end of which time the gold came out pure."[6]

The temperature needed for the smelting is 1943°F.

Peter called on believers to rejoice in the face of difficulty. It is a reminder of what Jesus said in the Sermon on the Mount:

> "Blessed are you when people insult you, persecute you and falsely say all kinds of evil against you because of Me. Rejoice and be glad, because great is your reward in heaven, for in the same way they persecuted the prophets who were before you" (Mat-

thew 5:11,12). In Greek the term "rejoice" means to "exult, to be overjoyed, a jubilant and thankful exultation…a term not used in secular Greek."[7]

The idea of this kind of joy was introduced by Christianity, surprisingly at a time when the world all around was seemingly falling down.

The context for such rejoicing was "now for a little while you may have to suffer grief in all kinds of trials." There are some who think that when they live for Christ, they should be spared suffering or difficulty, that they should always land on their feet, and life will have a musical accompaniment, but the Bible never encourages any kind of "life in Disney World" thinking. Nor does it necessarily mean that our suffering is because we are doing something wrong or faith is lacking. Life is difficult and when one follows Christ, difficulty takes on a new dimension. Drummond warned, "if you seek first the Kingdom of God you will have trouble; but if you seek something else first, you will have nothing but trouble."[8]

Peter's spoke of "all kinds of trials." We don't have the option to choose what difficulty we may face. Some who read this epistle would lay down their lives for the gospel while others would lose all they had. Some may have suffered from survivor's guilt in that they suffered no measurable loss. There is a wide range of trials that people face in their faith walk. It is foolish to compare what following Christ has cost us with what it costs someone else. The Bible counsels, "Each heart knows its own bitterness, and no one else can share its joy" (Proverbs 14:10).

God uses trials to prove the genuineness of our faith. It is wrong to think that God inspires sin in us in order to prove our faith. But God has a way of taking even evil and bending it to serve His purposes while not relieving the perpetrator's responsibility. Faith unproven is always a question mark. It is only by its testing that we can know where we fall short or where we find our strength to endure and overcome. We would like there to be a superhighway free of potholes and accidents but the best way forward for us is more likely a trackless swamp that demands the lamp of faith to get us through. Tested faith is more valuable than gold, Peter said.

With the trials comes the grace of God. We are not left alone though all around abandon us. We are not without sustenance though deprived of every morsel of food. The grace of God meets us at our most critical moment and carries us when the burden would pull us under. The testing is not to break us but to make us into something we could never be had we not gone through the trial.

Then Peter reminded them that their faith was already proven by their belief in Jesus Christ. "Though you have not seen Him, you love Him; and even though you do not see Him now, you believe in Him and are filled with inexpressible and glorious joy, for you are receiving the end of your faith, the salvation of your souls" (vs. 8-9).

By the time Peter wrote this epistle, the numbers were dwindling of those who had actually seen and heard Jesus in person. As the persecutions spread, the numbers would drop more dramatically. And these believers, spread as they were across Asia Minor, had almost no chance of having ever heard or seen Jesus. But they still believed.

The Church Father Oecumenius wrote, "If you love Him now when you have not seen Him but have only heard about Him, think how much more you will love Him when you finally do see Him and when He appears in His glory! For if His sufferings and death have drawn you to Him, how much more will you be attracted by His incredible splendor, when He will grant you the salvation of your souls as your reward."[9]

Facebook offers the feature that when a disaster strikes an area, someone can communicate that they are "marked safe." When you have faithfully served the Lord and have the joy of meeting Him, all of creation will know that you have been "marked safe."

## DISCUSSION QUESTIONS

1. What are some of the trials you have faced as a believer?

2. What does the author mean when he says, "The testing is not to break us but to make us."?

3. As someone who believes in Christ though you have never seen Him, what do you think it might be like to see Him in His glory?

# 4

# INTENSE INVESTIGATION

*Concerning this salvation, the prophets, who
spoke of the grace that was to come to you,
searched intently and with the greatest care,
trying to find out the time and circumstances
to which the Spirit of Christ in them was
pointing when He predicted the sufferings of
the Messiah and the glories that would follow.
It was revealed to them that they were not
serving themselves but you, when they spoke
of the things that have now been told you by
those who have preached the gospel to you by
the Holy Spirit sent from heaven. Even angels
long to look into these things.* 1 Peter 1:10-12

Occasionally archaeologists discover something that rewrites history. Such was the case when Antikythera Mechanism was deciphered. Found by Greek sponge divers in 1900, scientists were baffled as to what it was or how it worked. After great effort, they discovered it was a kind of ancient computer going back to around 100 BC. Able to precisely track the movement of the moon and sun with more than 30 precise gears, it predates any-thing comparable by a thousand years. "This device is just extraordinary, the only thing of its kind," said study leader Mike Edmunds of Cardiff University in the United Kingdom. "The design is beautiful, the astronomy is exactly right…In terms of historical and scarcity value, I have to regard this mechanism as being more valuable than the Mona Lisa."[10] Intense scrutiny coupled with the latest tools helped scientists peer back into the past to unlock the se-crets of this marvelous discovery.

As great as this archaeological discovery is, Peter shared that even greater scrutiny and curiosity surrounded the salvation that they were now free to access.

Peter said they "searched intently" using language that can mean a house-to-house search[11] or kneeling down to examine something carefully.[12] We can only imagine the impact it was on Isaiah when he foretold the suffering Servant in Isaiah 53 or the coming kingdoms that would be superseded by the eternal kingdom as seen by Daniel. Throughout the prophets and going back as far as Moses, there were bits and pieces, scraps and morsels that God spread throughout the Old Testament of the coming King. Inspired by God, each of the prophets recorded what they were told. But it is hard to imagine that having been given an important clue, a needed detail, that they wrote it down and forgot it. Peter testified that they did not. No doubt they not only explored the meaning of what was laid before their feet, but they also looked into the other inspired writings, hoping to weave together something into a whole. Their message was not only for them to deliver but had become integrated into who they were.

No doubt that having understood that their prophecies spoke of the Messiah, the anointed one of God, they were baffled how it would come to be that He would be treated so badly and suffer so horribly at the hands of the ones He came to save. Or when He came that anyone could resist kneeling before Him in worship. They had seen the hardness of hearts of those in their own generation but when God stepped into history, surely then people would act differently. Their hearts informed by their inspired message said otherwise.

Not only that, but the angels themselves "long to look into these things" (vs. 12). Although a great deal about angels was in the apocryphal writings, what was said was often contradictory or clearly inconsistent with the teachings of the Bible. Although some things were known about angels in the canonical writings of the Old Testament, there was a great deal that remained a mystery. How could we know for certain what was the full scope of their operations? One would think, since angels were in the presence of God, their understanding would far exceed that of our sin darkened minds.

Yet, as they watched the plan of salvation unfold and saw how it could take the most wretched and make that person into something entirely different, they saw an operation of grace that was not open to them. From what we understand, the angels that sinned against God and were cast from His presence were not given an opportunity to repent. No wonder the faithful angels longed to look into something so wondrous as redemption.

The generations before and the hosts of heaven observed with the keenest interest and most profound desire to what happened to the generation that

Peter addressed. First generation Christians' persecution and suffering could make them feel that they were the least favored among all of history's people. Instead, they were the most favored because theirs was the generation when salvation rolled out across the land and infused the human race with hope.

We are also a part of that generation. For us, salvation is not something longed for from the ramparts of heaven or dangled just out of reach centuries in the future. It is the present reality that means that the there is no sin so deep and no person so saturated with it that the blood of Christ cannot clean, forgive, renew to claim that one as a child of God.

Even now it is a mystery. Charles Wesley asked in his famous hymn,

> And can it be that I should gain
> An interest in the Savior's blood
> Died He for me, who caused His pain
> For me, who Him to death pursued?
> Amazing love! How can it be
> That Thou, my God, shouldst die for me?
> Amazing love! How can it be
> That Thou, my God, shouldst die for me?[13]

## DISCUSSION QUESTIONS

1. How does your Bible study compare with the intense search employed by the prophets?

2. Do you agree that angels cannot experience salvation? Why or why not?

3. Since salvation caused the prophets and angels to marvel, how do you marvel at your own salvation?

# 5
# BE HOLY

*Therefore, with minds that are alert and fully
sober, set your hope on the grace to be brought
to you when Jesus Christ is revealed at His
coming. As obedient children, do not conform
to the evil desires you had when you lived in
ignorance. But just as He who called you is
holy, so be holy in all you do; for it is written:
"Be holy, because I am holy." Since you call
on a Father who judges each person's work
impartially, live out your time as foreigners
here in reverent fear.* 1 Peter 1:13-17

The great holiness exponent, Commissioner Samuel Logan Brengle, gave this definition of holiness:

"A complete conformity in all things great and small alike, to the holy will of God; being at one mind with God in all the judgments of the mind, in the feelings of the heart, and in all the outgoings of life, agreeing with God's estimate of things.

"Holiness is that state of our moral and spiritual nature which makes us love Jesus in His moral and spiritual nature. It does not consist in perfection of intellect, though the experience will give much greater clearness to a man's intellect and simplify and energize his operations. Nor does it necessarily consist in his perfection of conduct, though a holy man seeks with all his heart to make his outward conduct correspond to his inward light and love. But holiness does consist in complete deliverance from the sinful nature, and in the perfection of the spiritual graces of love, joy, peace, longsuffering, gentleness, truth, meekness and self-control."[14]

As high a standard as Brengle outlined, Peter's is even higher. "Just as He who called you is holy, so be holy in all you do; for it is written: 'Be holy, because I am holy'" (1:15, 16). We of the Wesleyan tradition hold to the biblical priority of holiness of life in God's children. When there is clear instruction, such as exists in these verses, we are obligated to make sure we understand what is being said.

The call to holiness started with a negative command, "Do not conform to the evil desires you had when you lived in ignorance" (vs. 14). There is to be separation from the old lifestyle and values when someone comes to Christ. What makes that difficult is we do not know how ingrained those behaviors and patterns of thinking are until we try not to act and think the old way. It is especially difficult if those around us have no interest in living a Christian life and expect that we behave as they do. Just as gravity holds us down, the pull of sin is always downward, never upward.

Sometimes a believer settles into a twilight zone of wanting enough grace for heaven but not enough to interfere with how he/she lives life. The same jokes are told, "colorful" language remains, the rumor is repeated, the anger unabated. For Sunday morning the act is cleaned up a bit, but only until Sunday afternoon when the person feels they are on their own time. There might be the sense that things are not right but unless the Holy Spirit pricks the hearts and they heed His voice, the professing believer goes on living a contorted and tainted Christianity. Such a one is as much an enemy of the faith as any atheist as he lives a hypocritical and inconsistent lifestyle.

But if it is put aside, what is left in its place?

Peter answered that we are to be holy as God is holy. It is marked by several characteristics:

**Be alert.** The Greek language, better translated in other versions than the NIV, meant "gird up your loins." It referred to a man's long robe being tucked into his belt so that he could run faster. In modern language we might say "roll up your sleeves." Being alert involves putting aside loose thinking that gets in the way of our devotion to God. It means exchanging biblical standards for the world's standards in our inner life.

**Be sober or self-controlled.** The idea here is we are not to approach our spiritual life in a haphazard way. It means we need to get down to business with God, no more playing tag with the lifestyle we lead.

**Set your hope.** The hope is enabled by grace

so that we can become what God intended us to be. Our confident hope is that when the Lord returns, He will not find us embarrassed by what we have refused to become by yielding to Him but instead rejoicing in what He has made us when we are conformed to His image.

We are to be holy even as God is holy. Our standard is not someone else, nor are we in a race with other Christians to place better in some holy competition. Our holiness standard cannot be found in any tradition, custom or ceremony but firmly and wholly upon the holy character of God. "God is holy and the passion of His heart, held in poignant focus at Calvary, is the creation of a family of children who will in fact be like Him."[15] Further, Witherington says, "The proper way, indeed the only correct way is to relate to a holy God by being holy like God; in this world believers are to reflect His character, His will, His glory."[16]

There is no third option. Either we obey God to be holy or we disobey Him. To not seek to be holy is to turn deliberately against His expressed will for our lives.

It is to be demonstrated in "all you do" (vs. 15). Our everyday lives should give testimony to His

Holy Spirit's dwelling in us and working through us. We should love the lost as He does while loathing the sin that enslaves them. Our hearts should be moved by what moves His, our hands set to work for that that He would have changed.

While holiness can seem daunting, we need to remember that God would not place a desire in us He could not meet, nor set a standard He would not help us reach nor make a command He would not enable us to obey.

## DISCUSSION QUESTIONS

1. How would you define holiness?

2. What does it mean to get down to business with God?

3. While holiness does not mean we are perfect in every respect, it does mean we are wholly given over to God and filled with His Spirit. How does that fit with your experience?

# 6

# BEFORE THE CREATION OF THE WORLD

*For you know that it was not with perishable
things such as silver or gold that you were
redeemed from the empty way of life handed
down to you from your ancestors, but with
the precious blood of Christ, a lamb without
blemish or defect. He was chosen before the
creation of the world, but was revealed in these
last times for your sake.* 1 Peter 1:18-20

Imagine a group of doctors counseling a young
couple. All is not well with their unborn child. The
head physician speaks: "We have found that your
baby has certain genes that express themselves in

the child's development. He has the gene which tells us he will be a gifted leader. But we also found a gene shared with mass murderers. Combined, the two characteristics are lethal. This child will likely be so evil that he could eclipse Adolf Hitler. We can state conclusively that he will murder without remorse, enjoying the suffering of his victims. You will not only suffer by watching him, but likely be his first victims."

The stunned father speaks. "What about love?"

How does science answer a father's heart?

"There's a chance your love could make a difference. But are you willing to take that chance?"

Measuring his words, the father speaks again. "You may want him aborted, but he is our son who we already love. How can we destroy him? How can we protect ourselves while making no effort to prove what love can do?"

When Peter was writing to the Christians who were already being scattered, hounded, and killed in the first of the great Roman persecutions, he called them strangers. He included a startling bit of information. "You know that it was not with perishable things…you were redeemed…but with the precious blood of Christ, a lamb without blemish or defect. He was chosen before the creation of the world" (I

Peter 1:18-20).

"Before the creation of the world." The great plan of redemption was not an afterthought by God or damage control following the failure in the Garden of Eden. No! It was His plan all along. He was not caught by surprise. He knew.

Before that first day of creation when light and darkness were created and separated from one another, He knew what would happen. He went ahead with creation anyway.

When He breathed into empty dust creating man's living soul, He knew that what He was raising from worthlessness would reject the gift of innocence and purposely choose to sin. Yet He formed humans anyway.

He knew that in each generation they would find themselves immersed in evil, sinners by birth and pursuing sin with a vengeance. That they would look for any god, rather than the only One who was, would spend more effort building monuments to themselves than knowing the God who formed the building materials. But God created us anyway.

Despite the beautiful creation God made, He had to put it aside. Not because any of the animals were wicked. No. It was humanity, made in the image of God, that spelled the doom of almost all of themselves and the animals as well. God sent a flood destroying all but a sampling of each. How easy it would have been for God to leave Noah and his family without an ark. Instead, He allowed Noah's little family an escape from His judgment. Did any change result in how people lived, any consecration to holy living? The Scripture records that humankind still found it easier to wallow in wretchedness than righteousness.

There were troubles in Egypt. Their problems extended beyond the forced labor of slavery to include idolatry. Ezekiel 20:6 and 7 says, "On that day I raised My hand in oath to them, to bring them out of the land of Egypt into a land that I had searched out for them, 'flowing with milk and honey,' the glory of all lands. Then I said to them, 'Each of you, throw away the abominations which are before his eyes, and do not defile yourselves with the idols of Egypt, I am the Lord your God" (NKJV). But while still wet from the mist of the Red Sea, they built a golden calf, proclaiming that it was this piece of metal, not the Almighty God, that brought them out of Egypt. They then spent forty years showing how ungrateful, how apt to stray a people could be in the shadow of the pillar of fire, symbol of the very presence of God.

The prophets came. Each generations' sins layered on the wickedness of the previous one. They made it clear they were not interested in the God who had gifted them with the land of Israel. The kings, who were to lead them to the worship of Yahweh, instead led them into the whoredoms of a host of false gods. Warned of approaching judgment, they decided that worshiping the gods of the invading nations would appease them, further driving the wedge between God and themselves. When enemies surrounded the cities, battering down the gates, arrows flying over the walls, and they were starving through the cruelties of a siege, the prophets still found their words ignored.

Then God's blessed and beloved Son left His bosom for the cesspool that the world had become. Would He be welcomed? A handful would but it was clear that even these couldn't figure it out. What of the Magi? We hear of no change in Persia. What of the shepherds? Their voices were silent after their first night of praise and worship. What of the religious leaders in Jerusalem? They failed to see the star, to hear the strain of the angels' song. Herod, mocking the faith he was supposed to defend, used its truth to try to destroy in His infancy the only Hope of the world.

Jesus began His ministry. How strange as He walked among the people He created, rotting in their own depravity. People sought bread rather than blessing, release from sickness in their bodies than from their sins. Most would be indifferent while others openly hostile.

He knew how it would end. Heaven witnessed the dark heart of Judas calculate the worth of His Savior, settling on the price of a galley slave. Who would enter into the traffic of the buying and selling of human souls? None other than the leaders whose avowed purpose was to lead people in the worship of the God they now despised.

There was reluctant cooperation from a Roman ruler who thought a mere basin of water would absolve him of guilt, waved off the death of another Jew and hid in his palace from the annoyance that day brought.

Then Heaven gasped in wonder as the beloved Son was riveted to a cross with His blood, His pure blood, flowing as unchecked as the agony He felt. Nor did the earth's convulsing, nor the darkness of the hour, nor the words of a dying thief asking to be remembered stop the mocking crowd gathered, their hellish glee crescendoing over the groans of a dying Savior.

This awful moment was no surprise. He saw it coming. But God created the world anyway. He sent His Son anyway.

Why?

Why not abort this cursed creation before evil was lived out in successive generations, a repeated tragedy with an endless number of scenes and acts? If this was known in advance, why did He create us anyway?

It is no surprise that parents would love a perfect baby. But loving a child that was known to be a monster would prove what love is.

How could God prove what it was to love? By creating beings programmed to sing with perfect voices and praise with every breath? Such creatures would be easy to love. But what of loving beings who rebelled and rejected, who started out their lives already wandering away, who had no hope of goodness despite understanding what it was. Loving these creatures would prove how unconditional love worked, how expansive, unselfish and giving it was possible to be. Paul cried out, "But God demonstrates His own love for us in this: while we were sinners, Christ died for us" (Romans 5:8).

God knew what would happen and followed through with His redemption plan anyway because of the sheer power of His love.

He stays through the presence of His Holy Spirit. Looking, looking, looking for a heart grown weary from carrying an unbearable burden. Listening, straining to hear the whisper of a soul who has realized that this is a land of hopelessness and despair. Loving and reaching for ones in the coldest of starless nights with no hope of a morning dawn.

Yes, this is a polluted and filthy world, but He loves it still. Yes, we are a detestable people, hateful and arrogant, but He loves us still. Yes, we have broken His heart time and again, time and again, but He loves us still. And He has loved us "since the creation of the world."

## DISCUSSION QUESTIONS

1. What does the pattern of humankind's sinfulness tell us about our own?

2. What present examples can you think of that show humankind's continued disregard for God?

3. What song best describes your response to the unconditional love of God?

# 7
# LOVE FERVENTLY

*Through Him you believe in God, who raised*
*Him from the dead and glorified Him, and so*
*your faith and hope are in God. Now that you*
*have purified yourselves by obeying the truth*
*so that you have sincere love for each other,*
*love one another deeply, from the heart.*
1 Peter 1:21-22

In the early days of The Salvation Army in Jamaica, a visitor to the little town of Bluefields described sitting in the dark awaiting a meeting to start. "We see before and behind numbers of small lights dancing through the bush, these, we discover, are the lamps carried by the people to light their way to the

Hall. By the way, they serve a double purpose, for these are the only lights we have to light our building. Can you picture the scene? One minute the Hall is almost dark and then dozens of small lanterns are brought by the congregation, some of who(m) hold them whilst singing, in order to see the words in the song book."[17] Without each providing light not only for themselves but for others, there would have been no meeting.

After describing the need for a holy life, Peter expanded on aspects that marked the Christian life.

"Through Him you believe in God, who raised Him from the dead and glorified Him, and so your faith and hope are in God" (vs. 21). The writers of the New Testament constantly marveled about that grand miracle of Christ's death and resurrection. While we tend to restrict our thoughts about these events to Holy Week or perhaps the Lenten Season, it seemed that in every stream of thought there was the exclamation point of the resurrection. Here Peter reminded them that the gifts of belief, faith, and hope are firmly grounded in the death and resurrection of Christ. We would do well to be similarly struck by the impact of Jesus rising from the dead. One of the encouraging developments in contemporary Christian music has been the recurring theme of Christ's resurrection. Nothing we have as Christians can exist without it. Paul pointedly said, "If Christ has not been raised, our preaching is useless and so is your faith" (1 Corinthians 15:14).

Peter next spoke of obedience that naturally bears the fruit of "sincere love for each other" that comes with a command: "Love one another deeply, from the heart" (vs. 22).

The Christian life was never meant to be lived in isolation. While we can appreciate the devotion represented by monastic life, the idea of withdrawing from society to devote oneself to spiritual development is foreign to the Bible. We were designed by God to live in community, starting with the family, then branching out from there. We need each other, whether we like it or not. It is one of the strongest reasons for gathering in corporate worship. Although we have to have a strong personal, vibrant personal relationship with the Lord cultivated through individual prayer and Bible reading, it is not enough. We need to hear each other's voices, listen to each other's prayers, and share what God is doing in and through us. As an introvert, I have to fight drawing into myself; frankly, sometimes the sharing at church is a bit annoying. But I know that if I do not participate in it the damage to my own soul would be great.

Peter not only expected that believers share with each other, but he framed it as a command. Loving each other is what we are to do. In the romantic notion of love, we think that love must always be accompanied by strong, positive emotion. But love is more a decision of the mind than it is an operation of the heart. We choose to love and who we will love. When the emotion cools, our choice to love or not remains. Hiebert speaks of the Greek word that Peter used, *apagesate*, explaining, "(It is) the love of full intelligence and understanding coupled with corresponding purpose. It is a love of rational good-will that desires the highest good for the one even at the expense of self."[18]

It is not to be a grudging, "I love you for Jesus' sake" kind of love. We are to love deeply. The original Greek word for "deeply" speaks of stretching, extended to the limit.[19]

There are different ways we can look at that. We will naturally click with certain people, finding that we have a rich fellowship with them. But then there are those others who seem to get on our nerves by doing nothing more than walking in the room. Some have prickly personalities or there's something about them we don't trust. Sometimes we can't put our finger on it. There's just something about them. But fervent love is indiscriminate. If we are in the family of God, we are commanded to love all of our sisters and brothers in Christ *fervently*.

Another aspect of this love is that we have been set apart as a community, sharing a common destiny, a common hope, a common life. There should be no place on earth where a believer is more welcome and accepted than among the fellowship of believers. "So in Christ Jesus you are all children of God through faith, for all of you who were baptized into Christ have clothed yourselves with Christ. There is neither Jew nor Gentile, neither slave nor free, nor is there male and female, for you are all one in Christ Jesus" (Galatians 3:26-28). There is no room for racism, elitism, or class—only fervent family love. Like the lights gathered together in our opening illustration, in our gathering together our own light brings light not only to ourselves but to others.

## DISCUSSION QUESTIONS

1. If we are saved through a personal decision to accept Christ, why is fellowship so important?

2. How do you handle loving someone who is difficult to love?

3. Given the importance of fellowship, what can we do to include those who are unable to come to church such as the prisoner, the shut-in or those who are forced to work when worship services are held?

# 8

# IMPERISHABLE SEED

*For you have been born again, not of*
*perishable seed, but of imperishable, through*
*the living and enduring word of God. For,*

*"All people are like grass,*
*and all their glory is like the flowers of the field;*
*the grass withers and the flowers fall,*
*but the word of the Lord endures forever."*

*And this is the word that was preached to you.*
1 Peter 1:23-25

"The oldest plant ever to be regenerated has
been grown from 32,000-year-old seeds—beating

the previous recordholder by some 30,000 years. A Russian team discovered a seed cache of *Silene stenophylla*, a flowering plant native to Siberia, that had been buried by an Ice Age squirrel near the banks of the Kolyma River. Radiocarbon dating confirmed that the seeds were 32,000 years old. The mature and immature seeds, which had been entirely encased in ice, were unearthed from 124 feet (38 meters) below the permafrost...

"The team extracted that tissue from the frozen seeds, placed it in vials, and successfully germinated the plants, according to a new study. The plants—identical to each other but with different flower shapes from modern *S. stenophylla*—grew, flowered, and, after a year, created seeds of their own."[20] Life remained in the seeds despite the passing centuries. But although life in the seed remained, the plants that sprung forth will now eventually die.

While there is understandable excitement about ancient seeds sprouting to life, Peter shared that we are born again through "imperishable seed" (vs. 23). "The word Peter selects for seed is a rare word and it appears to have been chosen because it focuses more on the process of sowing than it does on the seed as such."[21] From this we can gather that the seed was not an end in itself but meant to grow and produce. We were born again through the sowing of the Word of God. Each of us owe gratitude to someone's faithful sowing of the Word for showing us the way to salvation. We, in turn, are to sow it so that others can find Him.

One of the current dangers even in evangelical circles is the widespread ignorance of the Bible. Although available in almost every conceivable format, translation and packaging, since the Reformation there has never been a time when the Bible was less read and consequently less heeded than now. And while nearly all believers would agree that the Scriptures are foundational to all we believe and how we are to be guided, there is a chasm between believing, reading, and study. Consequently, conduct suffers.

When believers are not attentive to the Scriptures, they become easy prey for those groups that claim to be Christian but at their core are not. Many of the things they teach look good at first glance, but upon deeper examination it is discovered that they stray further and further from what the Bible teaches. If a believer is not grounded in the Word of God, he or she can easily be led away by those who claim a newer revelation that supposedly "enhances" or eclipses the Bible.

What is of equal if not greater concern, is the gymnastics of those who would twist the Scriptures to bend it to their personal will, usually to justify a sin they find convenient. What is plainly said is explained away. Sin is no longer sin or was only sin because the inspired writers of Scripture were unenlightened. When we begin to chip away at the reliability of God's Word, we find all too quickly that our beliefs and practices are eroded as well.

That the Bible is banned or unlawful to distribute in many countries is proof enough that those outside of Christianity are well aware of its life-changing power. One of the boons of the Internet is that the Bible can reach places where carrying the printed Word is either dangerous or impossible. Because it is "imperishable seed" we can trust that it will do its work. We are reminded what God pronounced through Isaiah. "My word that goes out from My mouth: It will not return to Me empty, but will accomplish what I desire and achieve the purpose for which I sent it" (Isaiah 55:11).

Clearly, God's intention was for His Word to be fully operational at all times in all places in all cultures and in all settings. It is not to be sliced and diced, slavishly adhered to in one section while disregarded in another. Its whole testimony informs our living. The importance of the Scriptures is captured in a tribute to it by an unknown author:

> "This Book is the mind of God, the state of man, the way of salvation, the doom of sinners, and the happiness of believers. Its doctrines are holy, its precepts are binding; its histories are true, and its decisions are immutable.

> "Read it to be wise, believe it to be safe, practice it to be holy. It contains light to direct you, food to support you, and comfort to cheer you. It is the traveler's map, the pilgrim's staff, the pilot's compass, the soldier's sword, and the Christian's character. Here paradise is restored, heaven opened, and the gates of hell disclosed. Christ is its grand subject, our good its design, and the glory of God its end. It should fill the memory, rule the heart, and guide the feet. Read it slowly, frequently, prayerfully. It is a mine of wealth, a paradise of glory, and a river of pleasure. Follow its precepts and it will lead you to Calvary, to the empty tomb, to a resurrected life in Christ; yes, to glory itself,

for eternity."[22]

## DISCUSSION QUESTIONS

1. What are your personal Bible reading habits?

2. The author refers to groups that depend upon limited knowledge of the Bible to lead people astray. Can you think of any of these groups? If so, can you give an example of what they teach that is contrary to Scripture?

3. In those places where printed Bibles are banned, how can God use other means to reach people with the gospel?

# 9
# PURE MILK

*Therefore, rid yourselves of all malice and
all deceit, hypocrisy, envy, and slander of
every kind. Like newborn babies, crave pure
spiritual milk, so that by it you may grow
up in your salvation, now that you have
tasted that the Lord is good.* 1 Peter 2:1-3

According to the National Dairy Council, milk is
filled with nine essential nutrients that benefit our
health:

- **Calcium**: Builds healthy bones and teeth;
  maintains bone mass
- **Protein**: Serves as a source of energy;

builds/repairs muscle tissue
- **Potassium**: Helps maintain a healthy blood pressure
- **Phosphorus**: Helps strengthen bones and generate energy
- **Vitamin D**: Helps maintain bones
- **Vitamin B12**: Maintains healthy red blood cells and nerve tissue
- **Vitamin A**: Maintains the immune system; helps maintain normal vision and skin
- **Riboflavin (B2)**: Converts food into energy
- **Niacin**: Metabolizes sugars and fatty acids

In addition, milk has been found to reduce coronary heart disease and contribute to weight loss.[23] Milk is as close to a perfect food as there is for human consumption. It was fitting that Peter used the illustration of milk as an antidote for a list of nasty infections that can invade the body of Christ.

Peter commanded them to "put off," using a Greek term that refers to the removal of especially soiled clothing. Jobes notes that in the early church this metaphor was used to refer to ridding behavior that was inconsistent with the Christian life.[24] Witherington further notes that it would be a reminder of the rite of baptism when the new believer removed his old clothing, symbolizing his departure from the old life, and entered the river to symbolize his washing in the blood of Christ.[25]

The list of behaviors that cannot be tolerated are:

- **Malice**: Generally meaning anything evil or wicked.

- **Deceit**: The idea here is of cunning and treachery. The original word evolved from one meaning a bait for fish.

- **Hypocrisy**: The root word is from the theater where Greek actors wore masks as they changed roles. It evolved to mean someone who pretended to be one thing, but underneath was something else.

- **Envy**: The disposition to hate to see someone else succeed. It is almost always seen when someone excels or receives attention in an area where we feel we also have equal or better gifts or talents.

- **Slander**: The Greek literally means, "evil speech." It is the practice of constantly putting down others. It ascribes unworthy or wrongful motives for something that someone else has done.

In commenting on this list, Augustine explained, "Malice delights in another's hurt; envy pines at another's good; guile imparts duplicity to the hearts; hypocrisy (or flattery) to the tongue; evil speakings wound another's character."[26]

To fight back, Peter instructed them, "Like new-born babies, crave spiritual milk, so that you may grow up in your salvation" (vs. 2). Most commentators agree that the reference is to the Word of God as spoken of in the previous verses. The Bible not only informs but nourishes us in our spiritual lives.

It is important to note that we do not grow into salvation but grow up in salvation. The salvation of our parents or grandparents is not enough to save us as individuals. We don't grow into it by close association with other saved people. We have to have our own personal experience with the Lord.

The gift of salvation is outside of ourselves and only attainable by God's grace. But we enter into a cooperative arrangement with God's Spirit as He shows us what is lacking, where growth is needed, where He would lead us next. We are not simply saved and that is it. We continue to grow, to become what God intends for us to be. However, if we do not break with the behaviors such as Peter listed, we will find that we are stunted in our spiritual growth.

Sadly, there are far too many Christians who are stunted in their growth because they will not put these sins away. We have all struggled with not getting past real or imagined hurts from the past or being obsessively jealous of another's success. Maybe we could hide our feelings, all the while smoldering in resentment. Often, we are caught off guard by our reactions when we see someone else praised or used. We can feel left out or unappreciated. Rather than battling on our own, we need to flee to the Lord, asking Him to help us. It may be that we find it is an ongoing battle, but we are not left to fight it by ourselves. We are each cherished by the Lord for who we are and what we can contribute even if not another soul notices us or seems to care.

Perhaps remembering past struggles or realizing the presence of the sins mentioned has left a bitter taste in the believer's mouth. Peter reminded that they have "tasted and seen that the Lord is good" (vs. 3). The word that he used for taste is not some quick touching to the tongue but savoring and eating27. Our taste is our own, and what tastes good to us may be repulsive to another. We savor what tastes good and enjoy the experience of eating as a result. Peter invites us to taste in that way the good-ness of the Lord.

## DISCUSSION QUESTIONS

1. What do you remember about putting off the old life before Christ?

2. Which of the five sins Peter mentioned have you struggled with?

3. What does it mean to you to taste and see that the Lord is good?

# 10

# THE LIVING STONE— AND STONES

*As you come to Him, the living Stone—rejected by humans but chosen by God and precious to Him—you also, like living stones, are being built into a spiritual house to be a holy priesthood, offering spiritual sacrifices acceptable to God through Jesus Christ. For in Scripture it says:*

> *"See, I lay a stone in Zion,*
> *a chosen and precious cornerstone,*
> *and the one who trusts in Him*
> *will never be put to shame."*

*Now to you who believe, this stone is precious. But to those who do not believe,*

*"The stone the builders rejected
has become the cornerstone,"*

*and,*

*"A stone that causes people to stumble
and a rock that makes them fall."*

*They stumble because they disobey
the message—which is also what they
were destined for.* 1 Peter 2:4-8

Imagine you were tasked to construct a grand cathedral. You would immediately be beset by hundreds of questions that had to be answered before you could complete such a massive task. Where does the money come from and when will it be available? Who will design it? Who will be involved? How many supervisors and what levels? Where do you find skilled labor as well as those who will do the "grunt" work? Where do you find the proper materials and how will you get them to your site? Will you cut the stones onsite or have them shipped ready to go? What about the stained glass? What of the furnishings? And that would only be the beginning of the questions before you began, let alone the answers to be found when complications arose. When we see those majestic cathedrals that direct our eyes heavenward, they represent ten thousand thoughts and plans we could scarcely imagine.

As Peter wrote this passage, the gleaming Temple in Jerusalem stood in stately grandeur as one of the Seven Wonders of the Ancient World. But before his letter could be fully circulated in the known world, the great Jewish rebellion would begin. With it, that Temple would eventually be laid waste. If this great symbol of God's presence could not last, what could?

Beyond that question was one about the seismic shift within Judaism with the advent of Christianity. Was Christianity contained within the Jewish religion? Was it something separate? What of the tidal wave of Gentiles pouring into the ranks of what started with a decidedly Jewish base?

Peter witnessed this from the first breath of the Church's existence. A staunch traditional Jew himself, he was at the forefront of the change when Gentiles were included. He knew that nothing could be the same. Meanwhile, the Jewish faith as the vessel of God's revelation had brought vital ideas that must be incorporated into what was now emerging.

Addressing this, he spoke to his readers first about how they approached the Lord: "As you come to Him…" (vs. 4). The word "come" was used to describe a person coming to worship. This is not coming to Him in salvation but a continual, habitual coming to the Lord in prayer, to listen to what God had to say. Our faith is not a once-and-for-all quick answer to all life's questions. Things we could never imagine happen to us. Situations change. We change. We cannot go on with yesterday's answers because the present day demands new ones. So, we must come—to adore, to seek, to listen.

Then Peter took a sharp turn in one of the most interesting pictures of the church. The Temple was not that stately structure in Jerusalem. *We* are the new Temple, the dwelling place of God. It is staggering. His words must have sounded like a thunderclap, especially to those grounded in the Jewish faith.

This new temple is built on Christ, the living cornerstone. The idea was not new. The early believers seized on an Old Testament idea as found in Psalm 118:22, "The stone the builders rejected has become the cornerstone," and again, "So this is what the Sovereign Lord says: 'See, I lay a stone in Zion, a tested stone, a precious cornerstone for a sure foundation; the one who relies on it will never be stricken with panic'"(Isaiah 28:16).

Peter reminded believers that Christ did not on His own aspire to fill the role of Messiah. The idea of His substitutionary death and resurrection was not from some brainstorming He did either in Heaven or with His followers once He got here. He was chosen by God, as we read already, "before the creation of the world" (1 Peter 1:17). As such, He was declared to be "precious" to God. The Son of God was not some random heavenly being who was considered expendable. Quite the opposite. He was the one loved most dearly, most cherished, most wondrously.

Although that should have been sufficient for all humankind to immediately bow before Him in humble surrender, instead He was "rejected by humans." Sin so embraced humanity that as a race and as individuals even when God Himself showed up, for most it was not enough. Ironically, in their wholesale efforts to get around, minimize or deny Him they only found that He was to be a stumbling block. While the Savior might be rejected, He would not be ignored.

Peter called Him the "the living Stone." To us, there is nothing more devoid of life than rock. We talk about someone being stone deaf, meaning they can't hear anything at all. The contradiction of something as dead as stone being called living causes us to pause. Why choose this way to describe Christ? But then, what could be more dead than a beaten, torn and nearly bloodless body laid in the borrowed tomb on Good Friday? And what could be more alive than the triumphant, victorious Lord of Easter morning?

But wait! We also are living stones. Paul proclaimed, "you were dead in your transgressions and sins" (Ephesians 2:1). Lifeless. Stone cold. Dead. Then Jesus came and the least promising material, the most hopeless of cases, the most bewilderingly lost of people suddenly in Him became living, breathing, flourishing life!

And what happens to us now? He has a purpose for us. We are fitted together into a dwelling place, a temple for His use. Remember how the glory of the Lord filled the Tabernacle when Moses dedicated it? Recall how He filled the first Temple when Solomon dedicated it? And now He is coming to fill you—but not you alone. No stone sitting by itself ever formed a cathedral. We become His temple by doing so with others. Those who think they can live their Christianity in isolation are despising the building design of the Almighty God.

If you are in Christ, you are a living stone, being shaped for service to be joined with others who were in the same need that demanded the same salvation.

## DISCUSSION QUESTIONS:

1. In what ways do people either embrace Christ as a Living Stone or stumble over Him?

2. What does it mean to you to be a living stone?

3. The author says that we are to become God's temple in conjunction with others. Why do you agree or disagree with that statement?

# 11
# THE PEOPLE OF GOD

*But you are a chosen people, a royal priesthood,*
*a holy nation, God's special possession, that*
*you may declare the praises of Him who called*
*you out of darkness into His wonderful light.*
*Once you were not a people, but now you are*
*the people of God; once you had not received*
*mercy, but now you have received mercy.*
1 Peter 2:9-10

After the miserable failure of Saul as Israel's first
king, Samuel, the spiritual leader of the nation, was
sent by God to find a replacement. He arrived in
Bethlehem where he invited Jesse to join him for
a sacrifice. When Jesse arrived, he came with his

sons. Immediately, Samuel was impressed with his oldest, Eliab. First Samuel 16:6-7 records, "Samuel saw Eliab and thought, 'Surely the Lord's anointed stands here before the Lord.' But the Lord said to Samuel, 'Do not consider his appearance or his height, for I have rejected him. The Lord does not look at the things people look at. People look at the outward appearance, but the Lord looks at the heart.'" As Samuel went through in succession the remaining sons of Jesse that were there, he was puzzled that not one of them was who God wanted. He asked Jesse, "Are these all the sons you have?"

Jesse answered that he had one son who was out tending the flocks. "He sent for him and had him brought in. He was glowing with health and had a fine appearance and handsome features. Then the Lord said, 'Rise and anoint him; this is the one'" (1 Samuel 16:12). Not considered important enough to bring along with the rest of the family, David was a nobody, but he was the somebody that God wanted.

From the records of the era, we know that Christians formed the most despised people group in the Roman Empire. Their religion flew in the face of Roman standards by rejecting emperor worship, refusing to join in the wild parties and compromising practices of the day and insisting that their Leader who was killed was instead very much alive.

The first century church that rose up became the full expression of what God had started with the Jewish people. Judaism was intended to be God's witness to the world, a beacon leading the nations to the Lord. It failed miserably at this but even with that, the structures were in place to aid in the mission of the church. When the church was born, it inherited a rich tradition of ceremonies, symbols, the sacred Scriptures, and guidelines. What was missing was the Messiah who would draw all that together, making sense of every prophecy, ceremony, and dream of the Jewish people. The church that formed after His resurrection was not to replace the Jewish religion but to bring it to its full expression.

That most of the Jews rejected Christ was tragic. Nonetheless, in addition to the believing Jews who followed Christ, there were now believing Gentiles, a large number of which were slaves and the poor. To the outsider they looked like a scraggly bunch of nobodies. The Lord saw them as something else. In these beautiful verses, Peter assures them that they are the continuation of God's chosen people, they had become what Israel was meant to be.

In addition to them being a chosen people, they were a royal priesthood. In Israel, only the descendants of Aaron could be priests while through David's tribe of Judah was traced the royal line. When one king attempted to usurp the priesthood, it met with tragic results (2 Chronicles 26:16-21). But now God had declared His children a royal priesthood. This does not mean that we literally function as a king nor that we now take on the tasks of priests. It means we enjoy the status of the best of God's chosen service roles for people.

We are a holy nation that has but one qualification for citizenship—our standing in Christ. The Church Father Didymus the Blind, wrote, "Although we are from many nations, the fact that we have all repented of our sins and accepted the common will and a common mind gives those who have repented one doctrine and one faith. Where there is a soul and heart common to all believers, then they are one people."[28]

We are called God's special possession. We are amazed when we try to comprehend the vastness of space. Scientists tell us there are over 100 billion galaxies, each comprised of billions of stars and planets. On the scale of the universe our little planet is hardly a speck of dust. But God says that we as the church, not the wonders of creation, are His special possession. He esteems us of more value than the universe that shouts His praises as it blazes in all its glory. God used the term "special possession" for Israel in Exodus 19:5 and Isaiah 43:20-21. That the term is now used for the church confirms that we are the new Israel and as such inheritors of all its favor, promises and responsibilities.

We were formed for a purpose: to "declare the praises of Him who called you into His wonderful light" (vs. 9). "The church is to declare His praises, a word that means 'virtues' or 'excellencies.' As the church, our practice should be an advertisement of God's virtues. Our conduct should sing His praises."[29] For the believer, praise to God should be as natural as breathing. It was what we were meant to do and what will occupy our eternity.

Peter beautifully wrote, "Once you were not a people, but now you are the people of God; once you had not received mercy, but now you have received mercy" (vs. 10). We share a common heritage, speak a common language, share common customs despite being of different races and ethnicity, educational and socioeconomic levels, political views, families of origin or thousands of other variables. We are not peoples but a people. A people of God. Mercy marks us as His very own.

## DISCUSSION QUESTIONS

1. Besides David, what other biblical characters were nobodies that God made somebodies?

2. Do you agree with the author that the church is the new Israel? Why or why not?

3. When you read these verses, what are your thoughts and feelings?

# 12

# FOREIGNERS AND EXILES

*Dear friends, I urge you, as foreigners and exiles, to abstain from sinful desires, which wage war against your soul. Live such good lives among the pagans that, though they accuse you of doing wrong, they may see your good deeds and glorify God on the day He visits us. Submit yourselves for the Lord's sake to every human authority: whether to the emperor, as the supreme authority, or to governors, who are sent by Him to punish those who do wrong and to commend those who do right. For it is God's will that by doing good you should silence the ignorant talk of foolish people. Live as free people, but do not use your freedom as a cover-up for evil; live as God's slaves. Show proper*

*respect to everyone, love the family of believers, fear God, honor the emperor.* 1 Peter 2:11-17

When we served overseas, we settled into housing, paid taxes, worked, obeyed the laws and shopped as did the people who were citizens. Even though we did many things as they did, we sometime struggled to understand the accents, customs, and enjoy the range of food they did. We were required by the government to register, to have a work permit and entered each place with the understanding that at a certain point, we were to leave. We were foreigners and no matter how well we understood the country, loved it or the people, that would not change.

In this passage Peter returned to the idea that Christians were foreigners and exiles, pilgrims if you will. They were living in a world where they didn't fit in, obeyed laws and encountered customs that were foreign to them. How they conducted themselves was of utmost importance both as a witness and as a way to reach the lost. "Peter sees Christians as God's nation among the nations and is concerned with how the Gentiles perceive Christian behavior."[30] Peter warned them "to abstain from sinful desires, which wage war against your soul" (vs. 11).

The sinful desires were not only gross sins such as blasphemy, criminal behavior or sexual sin but could be a host of other so-called "lesser" sins. Pride, gossip, slander, hypocrisy as addressed earlier by Peter could be as damaging to the Christian's soul and his witness as more outrageous acts. When he speaks of sins warring against the soul it is not hand-to-hand combat Peter has in mind but a planned military strategy.[31] Our enemy has a long warfare planned to undermine who we are in Christ.

"Live such good lives among the pagans that, though they accuse you of doing wrong, they may see your good deeds and glorify God..." (vs. 12). We simply cannot control what other people say about us. Although they may hush for a moment, if they are determined to speak against us, they will be prepared to do so at the next occasion. But Peter is saying that we should live such blameless lives that their slander will be hollow when others hear what they say. Barclay notes that the word for "good" in Greek means not only good "but also lovely, fine, attractive, winsome."[32] A holy life is tremendously attractive even to those who have no knowledge of God. God infused all of His creation with good so that we readily recognize a beautiful sunset, healthy tree, or an adorable child. Even those deeply stained by sin can see a good, holy life and realize it is something of great value. People can argue against our beliefs and practices, but a holy life is the best proclamation for the Christian faith.

As Peter wrote this there was a seething spirit of rebellion in Palestine that would burst into flame during the Jewish Rebellion of 66-73 AD. Led by the Zealots, those who yearned for a Jewish state would fight bravely against the Romans but finally were mercilessly crushed. When the rebellion ended Jerusalem was once again a heap of ruins. Peter would have been very aware of the unrest and knew some of his audience would be sympathizers for overthrowing Roman rule, especially after the first persecutions broke out.

Peter insisted that part of our witness and responsibility includes good conduct toward the government. He told them to submit, a military term that described the obedience of a junior officer toward a senior one.[33] Noting that this should be at the level of the emperor and kings as well as the next level of governors, it is all the more startling since the depraved Nero was the emperor. Our obedience to the lawful exercise of government authority is required whether or not we think the officeholder is worthy.

There is a notable exception. When the government requires obedience that is in clear violation of the Scriptures, civil disobedience is in order. The Roman government said that each person in the empire had to kneel before an altar and say, "Caesar is lord." To this the Christians rightfully refused to submit. In more recent times, the American civil rights movement that defied discriminatory laws was correct because those laws were contrary to the teachings of the Bible. We are obligated to stop at red lights, but we are under no constraints to betray our Lord. What we obey and what we disobey must be as much of a witness to the goodness of the Christian life as anything we profess. Early Salvation Army pioneer, George Scott Railton, wrote, "In our work, as in war, daring disobedience is sometimes the best faithfulness."[34]

Peter cautions, "As free people, do not use your freedom as a cover-up for evil; live as God's slaves" (vs. 16). Apparently, some in the early church felt that if they were made free in Christ, they were free in all things, taking it as a license for self-indulgence or even crime. Nothing could be further from the truth. Martin Luther expressed it well: "A Christian is a perfectly free lord of all, subject to none. A Christian is a perfectly dutiful servant of all subject to all."35

The dignity of all people is emphasized in Peter's call to "show respect for everyone…" (vs. 17). Roman and Jewish societies were highly structured, each class feeling it was divinely entitled to look down on those who had not attained their level. The Christian faith brought a new standard of respect for all, dignity extended to the lowest. It found expression in the church when the congregation leaders might be slaves and the slave owners subject to them. As we shall see, it meant the elevation of slaves and women. Superiority has been replaced with servanthood in the kingdom of God.

## DISCUSSION QUESTIONS

1. In what ways does your Christian walk make you a stranger and exile?

2. Give examples of how for the believer "actions speak louder than words."

3. Under what circumstances would you feel you needed to disobey the government or other ruling authority?

# 13

# SUBMISSION TO INJUSTICE

*Slaves, in reverent fear of God submit
yourselves to your masters, not only to those
who are good and considerate, but also to
those who are harsh. For it is commendable
if someone bears up under the pain of unjust
suffering because they are conscious of God.
But how is it to your credit if you receive a
beating for doing wrong and endure it? But if
you suffer for doing good and you endure it, this
is commendable before God.* 1 Peter 2:18-20

"Slavery was an ever-present feature of the Roman world. Slaves served in households, agricul-
ture, mines, the military, manufacturing workshops,

construction and a wide range of services within the city. As many as one in three of the population in Italy or one in five across the empire were slaves… Slavery…was so imbedded in Roman culture that slaves became almost invisible and there was certainly no feeling of injustice in this situation on the part of the rulers. Inequality in power, freedom and the control of resources…As K. Bradley eloquently puts it, 'freedom…was not a general right but a select privilege.'"[36] The status of slaves as people devoid of any rights or respect is confirmed by Peter Chrysologus, "Whatever a master does to a slave, undeservedly, in anger, willingly, unwillingly, in forgetfulness, after careful thought, knowingly, unknowingly, is judgment, justice and law."[37]

Unlike American slavery that was restricted to the African race, in the Roman Empire slaves were drawn from all races, all socioeconomic and educational backgrounds. Some were prisoners of war, others sold by their families, while still others might have been kidnapped, taken by pirates or born of slave parents. They not only served in manual and heavy labor but as domestics, teachers, doctors and the military. Save for the ones who bought their freedom, or had it granted like successful gladiators, all shared a common fate of having no status nor right of self-determination.

Given their low standing, it was revolutionary for Peter to even address them. Some have faulted him and other New Testament writers for not condemning slavery outright. But had the early church done so it would almost certainly have been extinguished altogether. Slave rebellions were swiftly and brutally put down as witnessed by the one led by Spartacus that ended with 3000 slaves being crucified along the highway leading to Rome. By addressing them as people and not objects, Christianity began a process that eroded and eventually destroyed the institution.[38] And in addressing them, Peter recognized that they could choose religious freedom against a culture that demanded that slaves worship the same deity as their masters.

His first command is that they submit, a word learned often through bitter circumstances. But they were not to submit because the law said so but "in reverent fear of God" (vs. 18). Since they were slaves and likely to remain so, Peter gave them instructions on how to serve their heavenly Master while in the employ of an earthly one. Christian service is never restricted by circumstances, the day of the week or the tasks to be performed. As we are children of God in every moment, we are in His service every moment. Although we may set aside a time for worship on Sunday or agree to some area of service in our congregation, there is no time off from Christian service when the meeting is over. There is no retirement plan in the kingdom of God or a time when we get away from it all. This is not to encourage a workaholic mentality. Rather, when the opportunity for service comes, however it might come, in reverence to God we pick up the shovel and get to work.

Slaves were obligated to submit whether or not they were receiving just treatment. In our age of insistence on individual rights, which as citizens of a country we should, we need to realize that the same thing is not transferable to the kingdom of God. The word used for "beating" means to "beat harshly and repeatedly."[39] We may grouse when we are treated unfairly but Peter told slaves to bear up under abuse when it is repeatedly administered. While abuse cannot be tolerated in a family situation, it may be that we find in other situations abuse is continual. This is not meant to be an answer for all situations, but we may be in a place where our perseverance in the name of the Lord will make a powerful statement as to whose and what we are.

Peter warned that if we are guilty of wrongdoing,

we cannot claim that we are working for the Lord. Sometimes Christian employees expect special favor and treatment from Christian employers. Barclay notes,

> "There are still some people who trade on the goodwill and the sympathy of a Christian master, and who think that the fact that both they and their employers are Christians gives them a right to dispense with discipline and punishment...His Christianity is not a reason for claiming exemption from discipline; it should bring him under self-control and should make him more conscientious than anyone else."[40]

When the slave endured the suffering for the right reasons and in the right way, it was "commendable before God" (vs. 20). It is fascinating that the word in Greek for "commendable" is translated elsewhere as "grace." It might be better to translate it, "If you suffer for doing good and you endure it, this is grace before God."[41]

May it be that if our hearts are right before God and we are called upon to suffer unjustly, God can look upon it as grace.

## DISCUSSION QUESTIONS

1. How does submission work in unjust situations?

2. Have you ever been called upon to suffer unjustly? How did you handle it? As you reflect on it, would you do anything different?

3. How can we show grace in the fact of injustice?

# 14

# CHRIST, OUR PATTERN

*To this you were called, because Christ
suffered for you, leaving you an example,
that you should follow in His steps.*

*"He committed no sin,
and no deceit was found in His mouth."*

*When they hurled their insults at Him, He did
not retaliate; when He suffered, He made no
threats. Instead, He entrusted Himself to Him
who judges justly. "He himself bore our sins"
in His body on the cross, so that we might die to
sins and live for righteousness; "by His wounds
you have been healed." For "you were like
sheep going astray," but now you have returned*

*to the Shepherd and Overseer of your souls.*
1 Peter 2:21-25

In the last few hours of Jesus's life and ministry on earth, He met with His closest disciples for a private dinner. Although it was customary for someone to wash the feet of dinner guests, no one wanted to stoop to perform such a menial task. Seeing this, Jesus took a basin and towel and kneeling in front each of His disciples, washed their feet. Their pride was replaced with shame, so much so that Peter tried to wave Jesus away. "Lord, are You going to wash my feet?" Jesus answered, "You do not realize now what I'm doing, but later you will understand" (John 13:1-17).

In this powerful act of humility, Jesus gave Peter and the other disciples a moving example of service. But the hours ahead, filled with grief, passion, and tragedy, provided a drama as the world had never seen nor ever would again. Over the years Peter relived and reviewed those hours, remembering this moment or that one, comparing with the others who were there as they filled in each other's missing pieces.

In speaking further to slaves, he challenged them. "To this you were called, because Christ suffered for you, leaving you an example that you should follow His steps" (vs. 21). The word he used for "example" is the same one that referred to children learning their letters. Students placed a thin sheet of paper where shapes of letters were impressed on a wax tablet from which they were copied of traced.[42]

When we begin following Christ, we may think we know what the future will be. In fact, we do not. While we may have moments of glory as the disciples did when they shared with Jesus the transfiguration or walked beside Him at the triumphal entry, there will also be those dark moments like the agonized prayer in Gethsemane, betrayal by a kiss or the darkness of Calvary. We are to follow His example in the sunshine or the shadow, tracing His steps until they lead to the cross if we are to also exult in the ecstasy of the resurrection. "The example was not left merely to be admired, but to be followed line by line, feature by feature."[43]

Peter reminded them that the Lord suffered all that He did but He "committed no sin, and no deceit was found in His mouth. When they hurled their insults at Him, He did not retaliate, when He suffered, He made no threats" (vs. 22-23). What more powerful example could there be when, in response to the mocking at His bleeding feet, He cried out, "Father, forgive them, for they do not know what they are doing" (Luke 23:34)? All power available to Jesus was at hand so that He could instantly destroy His tormentors and scatter His enemies across the face of the earth. In not lashing out, He left a powerful example.

He then reminded them that "'He Himself bore our sins in His body on the cross, so that we might die to sins and live for righteousness" (vs. 24). Crucifixion was the means of death for slaves. In His dying that way, the Lord stooped down to the lowest, most despised and disregarded segment of society to share a death such as they might be sentenced to die. The myths of the gods of Olympus had no story to match this one. Those gods, as well as the gods of other nations, demanded that their adherents scrape and bow in humiliation before them. But here was God, humiliated and wounded for the people who tormented Him.

"By His wounds you have been healed" (vs. 25). Most of the slaves could run their fingers over their scars, painful reminders of their bondage. Perhaps this slave was stooped or that one limped from bones broken that had not healed properly. Their smiles showed their missing teeth, or their remaining eye closed in silent reverence. His wounds.

He was captured and carried away. He was bound and cast into a dark hole until they lifted Him out. He knelt down for the beating that left His back a bloody mass. His brow had thorns dig their way deep into His skull. His hands and feet were riveted by unforgiving steel. His side was pierced with an undeserved spear. The slaves knew what it was to be wounded. And so did their Savior.

Torn from their families and many far from their homelands, put into homes they did not choose and given tasks for which they may have been ill suited, they may have felt like caged animals in the market. Peter reminded them that they were not left unloved. "Now you have returned to the Shepherd and Overseer of your souls" (vs. 25).

Even if they were new to the Christian faith, they would have soon heard the beloved words of the 23rd Psalm, "The Lord is my shepherd…" If they had not at one time been shepherds themselves, all would be familiar with the shepherds who herded their oft scattered sheep, who fought the beasts that would take them as prey, who risked their own lives to rescue the lamb in danger. Their masters may not have cared one whit for them. But the eternal God gathered them as a loving shepherd and when life was cruel and masters heartless the Overseer of their souls gently carried them along.

## DISCUSSION QUESTIONS

1. In what ways has the example of Jesus spoken to you?

2. We have examined how this passage might have related to slaves. How might it relate to refugees? To prisoners? To the lonely and depressed?

3. What do you think of the Lord as your Shepherd?

## 15

# WHAT WIVES SHOULD DO

*Wives, in the same way submit yourselves to your own husbands so that, if any of them do not believe the word, they may be won over without words by the behavior of their wives, when they see the purity and reverence of your lives.*

*Your beauty should not come from outward adornment, such as elaborate hairstyles and the wearing of gold jewelry or fine clothes. Rather, it should be that of your inner self, the unfading beauty of a gentle and quiet spirit, which is of great worth in God's sight. For this is the way the holy women of the past who put their hope in God used to adorn themselves. They submitted themselves to their own husbands, like Sarah, who obeyed Abraham and called him her lord.*

*You are her daughters if you do what is right and do not give way to fear.* 1 Peter 3:1-8

Mark W. Merrill has shared five things that men wish their wives knew:

1. **We desire validation**. When we do something well, we want you to take notice and affirm us. We want our wives to be our number one source of validation.

2. **We desire respect**. We want you to respect our judgment. A man needs his woman to value and trust his opinions and decisions, even if they prove to be wrong sometimes.

3. **We desire conciseness**. Even though I need to listen to her (my wife) express herself, I really just want her to be clear and concise with what she wants me to do.

4. **We desire forgiveness**. When we ask for forgiveness, we want you to grant us forgiveness and not hold a grudge against us and continue to bring up our historical mistakes.

5. **We desire support.** I've said on many occasions that husbands and wives were designed to complete each other, not compete with each other. We need to know that our wives are on our team.[44]

A list like this would be unthinkable in the times Peter lived. The role of women in general and wives in particular was a far cry from what exists in twenty-first century North America.

While certainly not on the level of slaves, in many ways a woman was scarcely better off, her status largely depending on what her husband decided. In these days, and for far too many centuries afterwards, a woman was only known by her relationship with the men in her family. She was someone's daughter, then someone's wife and then someone's mother. There was little appreciation for her as an individual.

A wife dared not to make her own decisions.[45] Chivalry toward women did not exist.[46] When she married, a woman was to take on her husband's friends as well as worship the gods that he honored.[47]

What Peter did with slaves, wives, and husbands is establish a Christian version of the household

code, a common system at this time. The code outlined the proper conduct expected of people within
a household. Unlike the present time, the conduct
of one's home was not a private affair but a public
concern. What happened in an individual's home
was very much the business of the whole community. "Peter's primary concern was not to improve the
social status of wives, but to offer a Christian wife
a strategy that would enable her to avoid violence,
disarm the opposition of her unbelieving husband
and lead him to Christ."[48]

In a subversion of the prevailing culture, Peter
addressed women as free moral agents, capable of
making their own decisions regarding faith. The
implications of this were enormous. Karen H. Jobes
explains,

> The husband and society would perceive
> the wife's worship of Jesus Christ as rebel-
> lion, especially if she worshipped Christ
> exclusively. If the wife persisted in her new
> religion to the extent that others outside the
> household learned of it, the husband would
> also feel  embarrassment and suffer criticism
> for not properly managing his household.
> This could seriously damage his social
> standing, even to the point of disqualifying

him for certain honors and offices. Third, the wife's attendance at Christian worship would provide the opportunity for her to have fellowship with other Christians who possibly were not her husband's friends. Depending on the specifics of social expectations, a wife's conversion to Christ could potentially have far-reaching implications for her husband and family.[49]

Concern for this kind of situation was part of the reason Paul warned about the danger of believers marrying unbelievers: "Do not be yoked together with unbelievers. For what do righteousness and wickedness have in common? Or what fellowship can light have with darkness?" (1 Corinthians 6:14). But what commonly occurred was that one or the other spouse was converted after marriage. The answer was not to leave the spouse because of the newfound faith, but work toward their loved one's conversion.

Peter addressed this by counseling, "Submit yourselves to your own husbands so that, if any of them do not believe the word, they may be won over without words by the behavior of their wives, when they see the purity and reverence of your lives" (3:1-2). While Peter told women to submit to their husbands, he in no way implied that because they are women should they submit to any or every man. This applies only in the home. Nor does it mean that a wife to submit to do anything that is morally wrong.[50] As with civil disobedience, there are times a stand must be taken against wrong regardless of the consequences.

The answer is not to for the wives to become contentious or try to argue their husbands into the kingdom of God. Quite the opposite. They are to be such good wives that their unassailable behavior is a powerful confirmation of the change that being born again produces. William Barclay explains, "The silent preaching of the loveliness of her life must break down the barriers of prejudice and hostility, and win her husband for the Master…it is the submission which, as someone has finely put it, is a 'voluntary selflessness,' the abasing of self, and the instinctive desire to serve, it is not the submission of fear, but the submission of perfect love."[51]

## DISCUSSION QUESTIONS

1. In marital relationships, what does submission look like?

2. In many countries of the world the rights of women are severely limited. How is Peter's advice relevant for them?

3. Regarding their faith, what advice would you give a couple preparing to marry?

# 16

# WHAT HUSBANDS SHOULD DO

*Husbands, in the same way be considerate as you live with your wives, and treat them with respect as the weaker partner and as heirs with you of the gracious gift of life, so that nothing will hinder your prayers.* 1 Peter 3:7

In the previous devotion, we shared Mark W. Merrill's thoughts on what men wish their wives understood about them. It is only fair to share what he says concerning what women wish their husbands understood.

1. **Wives desire appreciation**. Bottom line: don't ever take her for granted. Be her biggest fan!

2. **Wives desire attention**. The first ten minutes when you walk in the door sets the tone for the evening. By giving her your full attention, it shows that you truly respect and care for her.

3. **Wives desire affection**. All women crave attention, no matter how long they've been married. Ultimately, physical affection reinforces that you're still in love with her.

4. **Wives desire patience**. Men, I encourage you to talk calmly and patiently through issues with your wife. If you don't, you will be in constant conflict; or worse, she may even shut down.

5. **Wives desire friendship**. It's important to be a man who will listen to her share her difficulties and then comfort and help see her through the trials. Your wife also wants you to trust her with your thoughts, feelings, and challenges in life.[52]

Peter's household code for husbands was understandably much shorter than that for wives. The groundbreaking impact of Christianity for women converts was much greater than for men (see Devotion 15). For example, if a man was converted, it was expected that all the household would follow. A prime example of this in action is the story from Acts of the conversion of the Philippian jailor. After the earthquake that freed Paul and Silas as well as all the prisoners, the jailor fell at their feet. "He then brought them out and asked, 'Sirs, what must I do to be saved?' They replied, "Believe in the Lord Jesus, and you will be saved—you and your household'" (Acts 16:30-31, italics added). In a similar way, in parts of the world where tribal cultures still exist, the conversion of the head man signals the whole village or even the tribe are to forsake their former religion and follow Christ.

In Peter's day it was common for men to be allowed great latitude in their personal conduct as it related to marriage. Initiation of divorce proceedings was entirely in the hands of men and at their whim. Fidelity to wives was optional. Depending on the income level, it was not at all unusual for a man to have a wife to keep his home and a mistress who met his sexual desires. Rendezvous with other women was totally at the man's behest. While the

Jewish faith held much higher standards for marriage, the influx of Gentiles meant that many came in with those assumptions toward marriage.

Contrasting the cavalier attitude that men had toward marriage, Peter counseled husbands to be considerate toward their wives. The word in Greek means "knowledge and understanding derived from reason and common sense."[53] Such consideration prevents the physical, emotional or verbal abuse of their wives. There is no excuse for a man ever to raise his hand in anger against a woman. Too often excuses are made for brutish and aggressive behavior. All people are expected to corral their impulses. Nothing that another person does removes the responsibility for self-control from an individual nor does a believer have the right to resort to violence, especially against a family member.

Being considerate also means that husbands are to look after the welfare of their wives and, as much as possible, meet their needs. This includes financial, providing security, intimacy, and sharing in household duties.

What is emphasized not only here but throughout the New Testament is that a woman has distinct and equal status as a fellow believer. Peter said, "treat them with respect as the weaker partner and as heirs with you of the gracious gift of life" (vs. 7). When he said "weaker" it did not mean their spiritual standing. It is a recognition that as conditions existed at that time, a woman was substantially disadvantaged socially, economically, and legally with respect to men. There also exists a general physiological difference. Pound-for-pound, men have 25% more muscle than women. "Peter is simply talking about a physical weakness, as is especially clear from the use of the word 'vessel.'"[54]

That God considers the duties of a husband and the treatment of their wives a profoundly spiritual matter is seen in Peter's warning of the consequences: "So that nothing will hinder your prayers" (vs. 7). Church father Severus of Antioch commented, "Nothing hinders the work of God like trouble at home."[55] The word "hinder" refers to the military practice of constructing roadblocks to obstruct the path of advancing armies.[56] It is clear. God cannot hear the prayers of a man if He hears at the same time the cries of his abused wife. The husband has an absolute responsibility, whatever it takes, to set things right in his own household.

## DISCUSSION QUESTIONS

1. How might a first century Christian husband feel about the changes he had to make toward his wife? How are twenty-first century husbands impacted?

2. When confronted with domestic violence, how should we react or intercede?

3. If a wife can win her husband to Christ by her gentle witness, how might a husband win an unbelieving wife?

# 17

# BLESSINGS FOR EVIL

*Finally, all of you, be like-minded, be sympathetic, love one another, be compassionate and humble. Do not repay evil with evil or insult with insult. On the contrary, repay evil with blessing, because to this you were called so that you may inherit a blessing.* 1 Peter 3:8-9

The monk Telemachus was visiting Rome when he unexpectedly found himself in the Coliseum where gladiator combat unfolded before him. Horrified by the violence, he finally ran into the arena where he urged two gladiators to stop fighting, as their actions amounted to murder. When they tried to fight again, he put himself between them. The crowd booed, then demanded he be killed. He fell beneath an onslaught of stones from the crowd and died. It would seem a useless death, but the Emperor Honorius could not shake the sacrifice of the monk. His example led to the emperor outlawing gladiator combat in 405.[57]

Having addressed slaves, wives, and husbands, Peter now gave instructions how everyone should behave. There are five virtues listed, all of which deal with how we are to treat others of the Christian faith.

> **Like-minded**: We have different temperaments, personalities, life experiences, goals, joys, and burdens. How are we to be like-minded with people who are so different from us? This is "more of a call for unity of disposition than uniformity of opinion."[58] Unity comes from keeping first things first. Our focus must be on the Lord and His glory. Different views of how to accomplish a given task is not only inevitable, it is desirable. We don't check our minds at the door when we enter church. But disagreements must be handled in a spirit of goodwill and Christian love.
>
> **Sympathetic**: When we show sympathy, we are putting aside our own feelings to enter into

the feelings of another. Barclay notes, "One thing is clear, sympathy and selfishness cannot coexist."[59] It cannot be done hurriedly or without thought accompanying emotion. In its fullest and best expression, it moves to action in a way that preserves the dignity of the other person while providing meaningful assistance and/or understanding.

**Loving**: While we are not to love our biological family less, when we enter the Christian faith we expand our love to include those in the family of God. The kinship that exists between believers is precious, worthy of cultivation. The priority of this love between fellow believers is emphasized by John: "Whoever claims to love God yet hates a brother or sister is a liar. For whoever does not love their brother and sister, whom they have seen, cannot love God, whom they have not seen" (1 John 4:20).

**Compassionate**: Compassion "...depicts a warm and tender attitude—an affectionate sensitivity towards the needs of others...Such tenderhearted, compassionate feelings toward the needy knows no frontiers and naturally finds expression also toward those outside."[60]

If we dare draw a contrast between sympathy and compassion, sympathy tends to be more spontaneous whereas compassion is more expansive and considered. Sympathy may make us feel we should do something whereas compassion will not let us rest until something is done.

**Humble**: Humility may have been the most difficult for the Gentile believers to comprehend. Humility and humiliation were synonymous. The idea of intentionally acting in a humble way rather than to be forced to do so was totally countercultural. Witherington shares, "In pagan contexts it means something like base minded, ignoble, low, mean—a derogative term. Here it is seen as a virtue. It expresses a character directly modeled by Christ and 'humbling oneself.' This represents a new quality of life which was introduced by Christianity into their Hellenistic world… Humility comes not from a low opinion of self but from a high opinion of God realizing how much believers owe God and are dependent on God…it involves deeds of service, not a craven attitude that denigrates self."[61]

Retaliation is forbidden. "Do not repay evil with evil. On the contrary, repay evil with blessing, because to this you were called so that you may inherit the blessing" (vs. 7). Repaying evil with blessing requires effort. But if we don't take that attitude, evil is not contained but spread further. An angry response or act of retaliation not only can cause real harm but erode out witness or do irreparable damage. We are to build, not destroy; heal, not tear down.

The most common response to insult is to return one. But in the family of God we are not to yield to our natural instincts but through the power of the Holy Spirit, rise above them. One of the things I learned early in ministry, joking insults aside, was that sometimes there was truth in insults, a criticism I might well consider. That being the case, thinking of my comeback negates any benefit I might gain. Beyond that, the verbal backhanded slap is totally contrary to the spirit of Christ.

We repay evil with blessing. The word for "blessing" meant to "publicly speak well of someone."62 Beyond that, Jesus told us to love and pray for our enemies (Matthew 5:44). We are to seek their positive good, and ultimately, their salvation. We do not seek to bless them in their lifestyle of sin but to see them delivered from it by the grace of God.

## DISCUSSION QUESTIONS

1. What should happen when Christians disagree?

2. What are some examples of the biblical definition of humility?

3. What is the worst insult anyone said to you? How did you handle it? How did that align with what Peter says?

# 18

# THE EYES OF THE LORD

*For,*
*"Whoever would love life*
*and see good days*
*must keep their tongue from evil*
*and their lips from deceitful speech.*
*They must turn from evil and do good;*
*they must seek peace and pursue it.*
*For the eyes of the Lord are on the righteous*
*and His ears are attentive to their prayer,*
*but the face of the Lord is against those*
*who do evil."* 1 Peter 3:10-12

In April 1990, NASA launched the Hubble Space Telescope. Roughly the size of a school bus, its orbit is high above the haze and distortions of earth's atmosphere, allowing it to peer 13.4 billion light years away. Its pointing accuracy is comparable to shining a laser beam on Franklin Roosevelt's head on a dime from 200 miles away. Its viewing accuracy is comparable to seeing a pair of fireflies in Tokyo within ten feet of each other from Washington, DC.[63] As amazing as that is, God's eyesight infinitely eclipses it.

Continuing his thoughts from the previous verses (Devotion 17), Peter freely quoted verses from Psalm 33 and 34. The psalms are songs of deliverance, celebrating the blessings of God in the midst of trouble. Given their present situation, Peter naturally inclined to these Scriptures.

"Whoever would love life and see good days…" (vs. 10) is an invitation to believers to prosper in their spiritual life. We should want our soul life to be abundant, our spiritual life exciting and filled with purpose. As children, our business was to play; but as adults, the action takes place on a battleground, not a playground. There's nothing wrong with having some fun, but that is one of the joys along the journey, not the destination. The conditions to the abundant life are challenging.

Interestingly, the first challenge is with the tongue. James observed,

> "When we put bits into the mouths of horses to make them obey us, we can turn the whole animal. Or take ships as an example. Although they are so large and are driven by strong winds, they are steered by a very small rudder wherever the pilot wants to go. Likewise, the tongue is a small part of the body, but it makes great boasts. Consider what a great forest is set on fire by a small spark. The tongue also is a fire, a world of evil among the parts of the body. It corrupts the whole body, sets the whole course of one's life on fire, and is itself set on fire by hell" (James 3:3-6).

Peter warned against speaking evil and being deceitful. Patterson notes that the verb used "suggests vigorous struggle men face in order to avoid speaking evil."[64] The evil can be seen in cursing, boasting, gossip, slander, hypercritical comments, and insults. Deceit would include exaggeration, lying, and misleading. Unfortunately, we all have listened to ourselves say things that we wished we hadn't. It is a struggle, especially in a culture that winks at deceit and encourages unrestrained speech, regardless how it might hurt another. One of the unfortunate developments in social media is people have shown a virulence in expressions toward a faceless audience.

The second challenge is to turn from evil. Hiebert shares the Greek word for turn "pictures the individual as leaning over and swerving aside to avoid an encounter with evil."[65] Unfortunately, some believers seem to want to see how close they can get to the edge of the water before falling in. Then when they do, they claim they couldn't help it—it was somebody else's fault, or they didn't see it coming. If we are vulnerable to certain temptations, we need to take reasonable precautions. The alcoholic should turn from bars; the porn addict should make himself accountable; the thief should not handle other people's money or possessions. We are not ruled by our impulses but fortified by the Spirit of God. To turn involves a decision of the will and a firm commitment to obedience to God.

Turning from also involves a turning toward. We are "to do good" and "seek peace and pursue it" (vs. 11). Doing good involves obedience to the known will of God as revealed in His Word and under the guidance of the Spirit. It is actuated in our efforts. The venerable Benjamin Franklin said, "Well done is better than well said."[66]

Seeking peace is not a wistful hope for calmness. "When it is translated, it means 'to pursue with malignity.' Peace is not to be accepted or even merely promoted. Peace is to be actively pursued."[67] Peace needs to be pursued in relationships within our families, our faith community and the world at large. Not that this means peace at any price. Peace does not equal being passive. There sometimes exists a state that, while there is not open conflict, there is a tense quiet which is anything but peaceful. We might find that we have to disturb the present in order to have real peace emerge. Peace, as the Bible defines it in the Hebrew word *shalom* means not only lack of conflict but a sense of wholesomeness and contentment. It can mean no less for us.

"The eyes of the Lord are on the righteous and His ears attentive to their prayer..." (vs. 12). Because God is omniscient, in truth His eyes are upon everything at all times in all places. But this is talking about God's attention being focused on the righteous. And because that righteousness cannot exist apart from a relationship with Him, it is the Lord as loving Father looking upon His children. When the sense of *shalom* mentioned above settles upon us, we rejoice when we think of Him thinking about us, and in His thinking, loving, regarding, caring about who we are and what is happening in and to us.

Contrasting that is God's reaction to evil. "But the face of the Lord is against those who do evil" (vs. 12). Sin and evil are repugnant to God. It has always been so, and it will always be regardless of whether we think something is tainted or not. Although David was beloved by God, He would not tolerate his sin with Bathsheba. It didn't matter at all whether David felt justified or felt nothing at all.

We choose whether we are in a place where the Lord can lovingly regard us, or where He turns His face against us.

## DISCUSSION QUESTIONS

1. What challenges have you had with your tongue?

2. In what ways can we turn from evil?

3. What does it say to you about God's eyes being on you?

# 19

# READY ANSWER

*Who is going to harm you if you are eager to do good? But even if you should suffer for what is right, you are blessed. "Do not fear their threats; do not be frightened." But in your hearts revere Christ as Lord. Always be prepared to give an answer to everyone who asks you to give the reason for the hope that you have. But do this with gentleness and respect, keeping a clear conscience, so that those who speak maliciously against your good behavior in Christ may be ashamed of their slander. For it is better, if it is God's will, to suffer for doing good than for doing evil.* 1 Peter 3:13-17

Elizabeth Geikie, a Scottish woman, followed God's calling in her life to serve as a Salvation Army officer in India. She knew she would have to dress, eat, and live as did the poorest of the Indian people. One night the villagers came to her hut with a man who was in agony.

Bending close to the litter Elizabeth Geikie saw a huge thorn driven like a nail through his foot; only the pinpoint was visible. Her medicine chest held only Vaseline, Epsom salts and castor oil, but if Elizabeth had no forceps, she had white firm teeth. Kneeling, she managed to clamp them around the thorn and wrench it free. Then she bathed the wound in coconut oil and wrapped it in clean lint.

Next day when the pain was gone, the villagers were curious to know more of Elizabeth's Geikie's God. Both the wounded man and his wife—though they never fully understood her sermons—became Salvationists. But they understood that to save a life a white woman had placed her lips, the most sacred part of the body, upon the most despised member, the foot.[68]

"Who is going to harm you for doing good?" Peter asked (vs. 13). The sensible answer is that sensible people will not. Obviously if they do, there is something wrong with them. And if the world always behaved in a rational way, then that would be the end of it. Christianity could continue on its course unmolested until everyone marched into Glory. But evil stubbornly holds the ground it has taken. To counter it, believers must stubbornly do good in the name of Christ. The Greek tense for "do good" is more than an occasional good deed but being zealous for the good.[69]

Peter warned them once again about the suffering they may endure as Christians, telling them not to fear it. He echoed what Jesus said about suffering, "Do not be afraid of those who kill the body but cannot kill the soul. Rather, be afraid of the One who can destroy both soul and body in hell" (Matthew 10:28). When Peter told them not to fear their threats, he used a term that means to "shake up or agitate, like water in a glass that is sharply jarred."[70] While God does not will that His people suffer persecution, He will calm their hearts in the midst of it, getting them through whatever they face. This does not mean God is a kind of fire escape when things heat up. Some die, are severely wounded, or lose all they have because of persecution. Rather, He will be with us as surely as He was with Daniel in the lion's den. Not only that, God uses suffering of all kinds to teach us that which we could not learn otherwise. Patterson reminds us that, "Human adversities are merely God's universities."[71]

"Always be prepared to give an answer to everyone who asks you the reason for the hope that you have" (vs. 15). The word for "answer" in Greek is apologia, from which we get the word apology. But he is not talking about asking forgiveness for what we believe. The original meaning of the word is a "rational explanation, defense."[72] We need to have such a clear understanding of what we believe that when asked, we can explain it calmly, sincerely, logically. We can't do it well if we think we will pull answers out of the air. Our lives should be a constant preparation for the critical moment. Groundwork includes reading our Bibles regularly and consistently—something more than the short Psalms or promise verses. We should also study the beliefs of the Christian Faith. What does it mean to be saved? How does God work in the world? Why do we believe the Bible is the authoritative Word of God? How is Christianity different from other religions? We may not be experts, but we should be prepared enough to hold a decent conversation. "Our faith must be a firsthand discovery, and not a secondhand story."[73]

If we are living consistently with our profession it will engender questions from non-believers. Some of these will be hostile, but most often, people sincerely want to understand what it is all about. Christianity raised questions in Peter's day and it still does today. It is our hope as individuals and the hope that shouts from the Christian Faith that prompts curiosity, especially in a day when there is so much despair, confusion, anger, bitterness, and loneliness.

All the more reason it should be shared "with gentleness and respect" (vs. 15). The Christian Faith may offend, but we should not be offensive in our presentation of it. Being obnoxious is odious even if dressed in religious garb. "It is exactly at those moments when a believer may feel the least like responding with a gracious testimony of hope in Christ that it is most important to do so."[74]

Peter returned to the prospect of persecution. In speaking of the assault that Christians may undeservedly suffer, he told them that the believer's good behavior is an unassailable answer. Such behavior causes them to "be ashamed of their slander" (vs. 16). The word for shame "connotes a social status, often related to utter defeat and disgrace in battle."[75] While we are being beaten up, we actually are winning when we are faithful.

Because of our faith, Peter's summary is self-evident. "For it is better, if it is God's will, to suffer for doing good than for doing evil" (vs. 17). If we are doing something wrong, we get what we deserve. If we are doing what is right in God's eyes, we are promised His reward, and our witness shines through.

## DISCUSSION QUESTIONS

1. If God does not will for persecution to happen, why doesn't He stop it?

2. How prepared are you to give an answer for your faith?

3. Peter was unprepared to give an answer for his faith on the night he denied Christ three times. What damage is done when we cannot stand up to questions about our life in Christ?

# 20

# RIGHTEOUS FOR UNRIGHTEOUS

*For Christ also suffered once for sins, the
righteous for the unrighteous, to bring you
to God. He was put to death in the body
but made alive in the Spirit.* 1 Peter 3:18

In 1989 a man bought a painting for $4 at a flea
market because he wanted to reuse the frame. When
he removed the lackluster painting, he realized the
frame could not be salvaged. But he found a paper
folded, hidden in the backing. It turned out to be an
original copy of the Declaration of Independence,
one of only 24 copies remaining. It sold two years
later at Sotheby's for $2.4 million, at that time the
highest price ever paid for a piece of Americana.[76]

Peter addressed suffering on several fronts, always seeking to have his readers understand the context of what they were undergoing. He wanted them to realize that Christ had led the way and His example provided their pattern for meeting persecution. He also wanted them to remember that, as pilgrims, their station on this earth was temporary and because of that, any persecution they met with was time limited. If it doesn't cease in this life, then they will be ushered into the presence of the Lord. Or the Lord will return and set all things right. Either way evil has limits, and as believers, they ultimately have something that overcomes the worst.

When I had a congregation to preach to, I noticed that while there might be general interest in most of the subjects I shared, whenever I spoke about suffering it seemed that the people were a little bit quieter, as if leaning forward to hear more. Suffering is universal. Our hearts are broken in relationships whether that be children with parents, parents with children, marital partners, or soured friendships. There are hurts that, though they may settle to a tolerable pain, at any time they can flare up and cast us down again.

There are the pains that come with changes of health and aging. Many agonize as they try to stretch money to cover impossible debts or fear a threatened or experience an unexpected job loss. These are very real causes of suffering, and we believe that the Lord provides us with the tender care we need in the midst of them. But Peter was talking about suffering that specifically comes because we follow Christ.

Peter reminded them that Jesus suffered first on their behalf. "For Christ also suffered once for sins, the righteous for the unrighteous, to bring you to God" (vs. 18). The early Christians were in the same danger that we are. In the midst of their problems, their suffering they could be so focused on their own pain that they could forget about the suffering of Christ. We will not be called upon to suffer to the degree that Jesus did, but in the midst of living our busy lives we can forget the cost of our salvation.

In the opening illustration we saw that the true value of the $4 purchase was unknown. But behind a battered exterior and hidden away there was a true treasure. It can be that in the politics of church, the hubbub of our lives, the noise that is constantly in the background we can form our own battered exterior that hides the treasure within. Going to church can become mechanical where we sing songs without thinking about the words, we notice the preacher's haircut or Mrs. B's dress instead of entering the beauty of worship. Prayers can be a string of cliched expressions that at one time meant something to someone somewhere but now are the formula used so we can get to the next thing on the program. All the while, the true value of what we believe, the beauty of the salvation that is ours in Jesus Christ is relegated to a ho-hum mental assent.

Peter never could forget the cross, never had it far from his consciousness. This was no abstract theological concept but a three-dimensional reality. He knew the color of Christ's blood. He had seen the scars that ripped His hands and lacerated His side. He had thought long and hard about the "why" of Christ's death. For me. For me.

Jesus, the righteous, had come for Peter, the unrighteous. He said, "You who are now suffering for Him, Christ came for you, the unrighteous to make you righteous. Even if you die for Him, you can remember that at one time you were unrighteous." He never was. The righteous for the unrighteous. What a profound debt.

"But made alive in the Spirit" (vs. 18). Had He died and that was it; He would have been a martyr, and an admirable one at that. But because He was made alive again, He moved from martyrdom to ascending to His exclusive place as our Savior. We didn't need a martyr. We desperately needed a Savior.

> When I survey the wondrous cross
> On which the Prince of glory died,
> My richest gain I count but loss,
> And pour contempt on all my pride.
>
> Forbid it, Lord, that I should boast,
> Save in the death of Christ my God!
> All the vain things that charm me most,
> I sacrifice them to His blood.
>
> See from His head, His hands, His feet,
> Sorrow and love flow mingled down!
> Did e'er such love and sorrow meet,
> Or thorns compose so rich a crown?
>
> Were the whole realm of nature mine,
> That were a present far too small;
> Love so amazing, so divine,
> Demands my soul, my life, my all.[77]

-Isaac Watts

## DISCUSSION QUESTIONS

1. Why is it dangerous for us to take Christ's sufferings for granted?

2. How do Christ's sufferings place ours into perspective?

3. How did Jesus' sufferings differ from anything we can experience?

# 21

# IMPRISONED SPIRITS

*After being made alive, He went and made proclamation to the imprisoned spirits—to those who were disobedient long ago when God waited patiently in the days of Noah while the ark was being built. In it only a few people, eight in all, were saved through water, and this water symbolizes baptism that now saves you also—not the removal of dirt from the body but the pledge of a clear conscience toward God. It saves you by the resurrection of Jesus Christ, who has gone into heaven and is at God's right hand—with angels, authorities and powers in submission to Him.* 1 Peter 3:19-22

This may well be one of the most disputed passage in all the Bible. Over the centuries, literally hundreds of views have emerged, many variations of variations. Nicholson notes that the different interpretations fall roughly into six categories:

1. Christ, in His preincarnate state, preached to the spirits in prison. This was done by the Holy Spirit in the preaching of Noah and his family who believed and were saved.

2. He preached to the victims of the Flood, who turned to God before they perished in the mighty waters of the Deluge.

3. He went in His Spirit into the realm where only spirits could go and proclaimed the righteousness of their judgment because they did not believe the preaching of Noah.

4. He went in the power of the Spirit and proclaimed Himself Victor and let the Old Testament saints ("prisoners of hope," Zechariah 9:12) on high, thus separating the paradise section of Hades from that of the wicked spirits.

5. He went in the non-corporeal (non-bodily) mode of His existence, upon which He entered

immediately after His death and proclaimed victory over the defiant and destructive fallen angels whose seductive power polluted the antediluvian (before the Flood) world and caused the Flood. His proclamation of victory over all evil was bad news for the evil spirits.

6. He went in His Spirit, not bodily form, between His crucifixion and resurrection and proclaimed the gospel message to set free those who once were disobedient but believed on Him after their death.[78]

The only way that Peter could have known about this was for him to learn it from Jesus directly following His resurrection. It would not be surprising that the disciples asked Jesus what happened between His physical death on the cross and His glorious resurrection on Sunday morning. It would seem that Peter was giving some sort of summary that perhaps was augmented by an oral tradition. Scholars note that both here and in the books of 2 Peter and Jude, there seems to be some reliance on the apocryphal book of 2 Enoch, but even this brief mention does not directly match that source.

In the end, we simply do not know for sure what happened, what the purpose was or the end result or for that matter, what it all means. It is truly a mystery.

We often wonder why God has done this or that, or what could be the possible outcome of something that raises questions in our minds and hearts. But we may need to accept that there are simply things that, if even given an explanation, we still would not understand. Our faith demands that we live with a certain degree of mystery. First of all, God is not accountable to us and owes us no explanation for His actions. Secondly, even if He explained it, as He has through His Word in this instance, it would be beyond our comprehension.

Suppose I take my dog to watch a space launch at Cape Canaveral. In preparation, I could show him all sorts of videos, let him see models of spacecraft, try to make some of the sounds of the spacecraft as it lifts into the air. On the trip, I could give him a lecture on rocket design, propulsion, the speed it must travel to escape earth's gravitational pull, the tasks the satellite is to perform, and the overall benefits for humanity. Then, reaching Cape Canaveral, I could tell my dog that he needed to look to the east for the launch. I can predict that when the flames of the rocket flash across the sky, my dog would be totally unimpressed. But when a few seconds later, the ground began to shake from the thrust of the engines, my little dog would be startled. That would be the sum total of my dog's comprehension. No amount of preparation or explanation was sufficient to help my dog understand what was happening.

Our puny brains can only understand so much. Even if God gave an explanation for everything He has done for us, is doing in us, has in store, and how that relates to the others in our lives, we would be unable to comprehend it. To be sure, He has given us brains that can understand a great deal; but, in the end, if we don't understand God's ways, it is because we are humans, long-term victims of the Fall whose full understanding has been darkened.

In Scripture, it does not seem that God is bothered that we ask questions. A prime example is Job, who in his suffering indulged himself with question after question about what God was doing and why he was going through his tribulation. At the end of the book, God turned the tables and asked Job a series of questions—not that He expected answers, but to prove to Job there was a wide host of things about which he hadn't a clue. In all of that, God did not offer one word of explanation of what had happened to Job.

That from time to time when we feel anger, discouragement, confusion it means that we are human. It is natural to question. But, like Job, we find that hurtling questions at God does not mean He has to answer us. It is true that there are times in retrospect we can see how God's actions brought us to the place where we needed to be, whether that was geographically, provisionally, or in our souls. There are likely many more that will puzzle us, for which we can make neither heads nor tails.

We live with mystery. We live in faith.

## DISCUSSION QUESTIONS

1. Which one of the six positions Nicholson outlines seems to you to be closest to being right? Why?

2. Think of something in your life that you have never understood. Describe your faith journey related to it.

3. Do you believe that we have to live with a certain amount of mystery? Why or why not?

## 22

# DONE WITH SIN

*Therefore, since Christ suffered in His body, arm
yourselves also with the same attitude, because
whoever suffers in the body is done with sin. As
a result, they do not live the rest of their earthly
lives for evil human desires, but rather for the
will of God. For you have spent enough time
in the past doing what pagans choose to do—
living in debauchery, lust, drunkenness, orgies,
carousing and detestable idolatry.* 1 Peter 4:1-3

H. A. Ironside was a great biblical preacher and writ-
er, serving for many years at Moody Church in Chicago. He started in ministry as a Salvation Army officer.
One of the most vivid memories from that time was of

a particular conversion and spectacular testimony.

In San Diego, a young girl was converted in an Army meeting. Her father, a good man but one who had no time for Christianity, owned a saloon. He noticed the change in his daughter's life and eventually came to a Salvation Army meeting. He came forward at the end of the meeting to accept Christ as Savior.

He was immediately struck by how his newfound faith was in direct opposition to his vocation. Friends counseled him to sell his saloon and use the money to set up another business. He would have nothing of it, feeling that to do so would not rid the city of what he now considered to be a gateway to hell. He went to the city authorities and got permission for an incredible demonstration of the change in his life.

At the intersection of four streets and with The Salvation Army band and Salvationists circling, he stacked a pyramid of beer barrels rolled out from his saloon. He stood on top of the mountain of booze, giving testimony to the change Christ had wrought in his life and urging those in the large crowd that had gathered to do so as well. Then, pouring bottle after bottle of liquor on the pyramid, he set fire to the whole thing accompanied by victory songs from the Army band.[79]

Peter counseled the believers that, in view of

Christ's sufferings, they were to "arm themselves with the same attitude" (vs. 1). They were urged to put on armor just as Paul had challenged in Ephesians 6:11-18. Those in armor are not involved in guerilla warfare but pitched battle. This was to be a deliberate and fierce, up-close fighting with the foe. They were to be armed with the attitude of Christ, who met evil face-to-face in all its ferocity and through His death and resurrection, wrestled it to the ground until it was utterly defeated.

"Whoever suffers in the body is done with sin" (vs. 1). When we suffer, we are sharply focused on the source of our pain as well as what is behind it. We are not interested in talking about the weather, our plans for vacation next year, or who did what to whom. When we suffer for Christ, we are so focused on the pain and why we are doing so in His name that we cannot entertain any sin. It is simply not within our field of vision. In a resounding note of victory, like the former saloon owner, we are done with sin.

Barclay shares, "There is a strong line in Jewish thought that suffering is in itself a great purifier, that, as the fire purifies gold, so suffering purifies the soul."[80] If a person is not fully given over to the Lord, when the suffering comes he will demand release from it, even if it means renouncing his faith. But the believer who sincerely loves the Lord with all of his or her heart, will find that any base desires are pushed aside in favor of his sincere desire to be worthy of suffering for Jesus' sake.

God promises, "I will forgive their wickedness and will remember their sins no more" (Hebrews 8:12). While He may not remember them, sometimes we are wise to recall what our life was without Christ. Peter does so when he said, "do not live the rest of their earthly lives for evil human desires, but rather for the will of God. For you spent enough time in the past doing what pagans choose to do— living in debauchery, lust, drunkenness, orgies, carousing and detestable idolatry" (vs. 2-3).

Almost all liquor and beer commercials totally avoid the problems that alcohol does to the human body or the toll it wreaks on society by those driving under the influence, the human cost of families wrecked, or lives left in ruins. Instead, they show how much fun you can have, how witty, and by implication, how dull your life is without it. Holy living, by contrast, looks dreadfully dull and a waste of time. That is how Christians appeared to their former associates in Peter's time just like the present.

Peter reminded them of what it looked like.

Debauchery refers to "excesses of the worst kinds of evils, involving a lack of self-restraint."

Lust involved "depraved cravings and inner vicious desires of fallen human nature." Drunkenness is just what it sounds like.[81]

"Orgies" generally meant "festive gatherings, merrymakings, revelries, either private or public and religious."[82] The most notorious of these were those in honor of the Roman god, Bacchus, with a festival called Bacchanalia. Bacchus was the god of wine and fertility. The annual celebration in his honor was attended originally by only women, but when men were admitted it degenerated into times of unrestrained drinking and sexual excesses involving group sex (orgies) with all ages and classes.[83]

Carousing referred to drinking parties.[84]

"Detestable idolatry" was more than the worship of false gods, but included its related practices, often with temple prostitutes and other base behavior that happened within the pagan temples.[85]

Peter did not remind the believers of these things to shame them but to remind them of what life without Christ was. They knew that all of these excesses had a steep price, that the moments of thoughtless indulgence were followed by hours of regret and damage repair. There comes a time when the party girl or guy looks pathetic, when the sexual adventurer is a disgusting leech.

As has been often, "I may not be all that I should be, but I thank God I am not what I used to be."

## DISCUSSION QUESTIONS

1. How do you arm yourself for spiritual battle?

2. What are the dangers to those whose lives are not fully given to the Lord?

3. In what ways does our present culture encourage the sins listed by Peter?

# 23

# SURPRISE TO SINNERS

*They are surprised that you do not join them
in their reckless, wild living, and they heap
abuse on you. But they will have to give
account to Him who is ready to judge the
living and the dead. For this is the reason
the gospel was preached even to those
who are now dead, so that they might be
judged according to human standards in
regard to the body, but live according to
God in regard to the spirit.* 1 Peter 4:4-6

Throughout history, there have been dictators who
have risen to power and then lost it all. With great
skill, they have manipulated the masses while at the

same time accomplishing some remarkable achievements. While they were oppressing others, those who shared leadership with him enjoyed lavish lifestyles, unchallenged power and a feeling that they were invincible.

History often documents how they seemed to be in the right at first. But over time, and with multiple atrocities committed, their regimes fell, often at the end of a long war. Stripped of all the accoutrements of power, the leaders were forced to account for what they did. Their former glory could not protect them from their final judgment.

In this section, Peter further addressed the ongoing concern with how the believers dealt with non-believers. He notes, "They are surprised you do not join them in their reckless, wild living and they heap abuse on you" (vs. 4). The Greek for "surprised" literally means "staggered by surprise" while "wild living" is the same terminology Jesus used when speaking about the lifestyle of the Prodigal Son.[86]

When someone is saved, it is not uncommon for unconverted friends to wonder what's wrong with them. Often, they hope what happened to their old friend will pass and they'll get back to "normal." The change in behavior creates in unbelieving friends a sense of things being out of balance. It is human nature that when things are out of balance, we do what we can to restore balance. Often, the unsaved friends will try to pull their old friend back into the lifestyle they shared. Or it might be that the new believer is sabotaged or simply attacked in anger. That is why when someone who has been addicted tries to live a sober life, he is often counseled to find new friends or not to return to the places where he knows the temptations to fall back into abuse are likely to occur. A righteous life is a constant rebuke to those who choose to live for themselves.

Peter warned, "But they will have to give account to Him who is ready to judge the living and the dead" (vs. 5). At God's judgment at the end of the world, all people will be called to account. Their former standing, power, prestige or wealth will provide no shelter when called before the Almighty God to account for how they lived their lives.

The idea of judgment, which includes condemnation, is an immensely unpopular subject, even among some believers. We'd like to think that because God is love, He will overlook any indiscretions. It is the hope of many that because most of what they did was, by their personal standard, "good" that it will appear so to God as well. The Bible paints a very different picture.

In the mercy of God, we believe that He will lovingly receive into His kingdom children who have died before they were old enough to realize the meaning of sin and salvation as well as adults whose mental capacity is so limited that they are prevented from having a concept of their sin and need for a Savior. This represents a very small part of the population.

Everyone else has a choice to make and, for most, decades to consider what they will do with the salvation offered through Christ. While it is granted that many will not have entered a church, passing a church is passing an opportunity to know more about God. With the proliferation of Christian radio and television stations, the ready availability of Bibles, Christian books and other literature, the tens of thousands of internet sites dedicated to share the gospel, and with most knowing someone who is a believer, there is little excuse for someone saying they had no opportunity.

What will that judgment look like?

There is an immediate judgment upon death when each person knows whether or not they have lived as they ought by God's standard. Then there is the general judgment at the conclusion of the age. *The Evangelical Dictionary of Theology* outlines aspects of God's judgment as seen through His judgment in the story of Noah's flood:

1. God's judgments are never arbitrary.

2. God can be counted on to judge sin.

3. God always gives sinners an opportunity to repent before judging them.

4. God always follows through on His decision to judge.

5. God judgments always lead to death.

6. God's judgments always include elements of both justice and grace.[87]

For a time, God has tolerated the presence of sin on the earth, but He will not tolerate it in His presence in eternity. Those who hold to their sins have chosen to use a boulder for a life preserver.

As Jobes observes, "The universal claim to truth was as offensive to first century Greco-Roman thought as it has become in today's pluralistic culture."[88] Whether it is hard for people to swallow or not, it is God's truth; and if we believe it at all, we ought to pray for all our loved ones, friends, neighbors, enemies—everyone—to find the Lord as Savior at the earliest possible moment.

## DISCUSSION QUESTIONS

1. How does being a Christian define our relationships with non-believers?

2. Why must we accept God's judgment upon those who do not receive Christ in this lifetime?

3. In what ways do God's judgments testify to His righteousness?

# 24

# SHARING LOVE

*The end of all things is near. Therefore, be
alert and of sober mind so that you may pray.
Above all, love each other deeply, because
love covers over a multitude of sins. Offer
hospitality to one another without grumbling.
Each of you should use whatever gift you have
received to serve others, as faithful stewards
of God's grace in its various forms. If anyone
speaks, they should do so as one who speaks
the very words of God. If anyone serves, they
should do so with the strength God provides, so
that in all things God may be praised through
Jesus Christ. To Him be the glory and the
power for ever and ever. Amen.* 1 Peter 4:7-11

After speaking about judgment for the unbeliev-er, Peter announced, "The end is near. Therefore, be alert and of sober mind so you may pray" (vs. 7). Over twenty centuries have passed since Peter wrote this. Had he gotten things wrong about the end being near? Not necessarily. Announcing that the end is near is not the same as saying it is right now. Rather, it means we have entered the last age before God establishes His kingdom on earth. Christ was the total revelation of all that God wanted to show and say to us. The present age is bookended by Christ's first and second coming.

In order to pray more effectively, Peter told them to be alert and sober-minded.[89] Prayer approached in this way is not "based on daydreams and unreal-ity, not the prayer based on surprised desperation, but the prayer that calls upon and submits to God in the light of the reality seen from God's perspective and thus obtains power and guidance in the situa-tion, however evil the time may be."[90]

Next, Peter challenged the believers, "Above all, love each other deeply, because love covers a multi-tude of sins" (vs. 8). A fighting couple decided that they had had enough of arguing. They agreed to sit down at a table and on a sheet of paper, each would list his/her grievances against the other. The husband glared at his wife, then wrote something. She immediately wrote something as well. Every time she stopped writing he would write some more. Finally, they stopped. The husband said, "Let's exchange our lists now." When she saw what he had written, she begged to take her list back. He had simply written, "I love you. I love you. I love you."[91]

The kind of love Peter was talking about is more than emotion. It is steadfast when all is going against it. It has no saving benefit, although he said it covers a multitude of sins. Only Christ's blood can wash away sin. Instead, it means that this kind of love remains strong in spite of the faults and foibles of another because there is supreme regard and interest in the other person. To deny shortcomings is neither realistic nor loving. The most loving thing to do often is to confront gently. But it also means that some things are just not worth the bother. An idiosyncrasy might even add color even though it can also be a bit irritating.

Judging from the command to love as well as various mentions of it in the epistles of Paul and John, one of the persistent problems in the early church was a spirit of division that led to bickering and grudges. In challenging them to love deeply, Peter used terminology that was used for a horse at full gallop or an athlete's muscles straining as he competes with all he has.[92]

Part of that love included hospitality. In ancient time, inns were notorious as fronts for prostitution. Beyond that, the custom of the day included offering food and shelter to a traveler. There was no thought as to whether the host liked the person, or it was convenient to have them or if resources were stretched. This especially became important as persecutions spread and Christians became refugees because they had to leave their homes.[93] Clement of Alexandria said that hospitality was akin to love.[94]

While in the present age it might not be practical to open one's home to strangers, there are other ways of showing hospitality. Making sure the visitor to church is welcomed and attended to, sharing a meal with a homeless person or speaking to someone who is visibly upset are ways we can show hospitality.

Peter moved to the exercise of gifts. Hiebert defines gifts as "any capacity that can be used for the benefit of the church."[95] As when Jesus spoke in the Parable of the Talents (Matthew 25:14-30), gifts of any kind are entrusted to us to use, not for ourselves but for the glory of God. As in the parable, we are to invest our gift for the glory of God, not deny or hide it because of the obligation it might place upon us.

Peter spoke about the gift of speaking. Powers expands the usual definition of the word, saying, "(It) often designates public activities like preaching and teaching. But it includes a wide array of other verbal activities such as singing and sharing words of praise and testimony in community gatherings or in ministering to the sick and in private conversation."[96]

Serving was another gift cited. The Greek word used is the one from which we get the English "deacon," originally signifying someone who waited on tables.[97] While some have a heart and a gift for service, all are called to serve. We acknowledge that some may have better perception for the best way to serve or who needs our service.

This does not mean that we cannot derive benefit from the giftedness. A gifted speaker can make his living as a preacher; a gifted singer can have a career of performing. The temptation with any kind of exceptional gift is to believe the flattery is all true and that the gift makes one person superior to another. Worse yet, that the one with the gift thinks she is the owner of it. Church father Barulio of Saragossa commented, "…the manifold grace of God is dispensed when the gift received is believed to belong also to the one who does not have it and when it is believed to have been given for the sake of him with whom it is shared."[98]

## DISCUSSION QUESTIONS

1. How should we regard the Second Coming of Christ?

2. What ways can you show hospitality?

3. What is your gift and how do you use it for God's glory?

# 25
## FIERY ORDEAL

*Dear friends, do not be surprised at the fiery
ordeal that has come on you to test you, as
though something strange were happening to
you. But rejoice inasmuch as you participate
in the sufferings of Christ, so that you may
be overjoyed when His glory is revealed.
If you are insulted because of the name of
Christ, you are blessed, for the Spirit of glory
and of God rests on you.* 1 Peter 4:12-14

On February 12, 2015 the Islamic State behead-
ed 21 Coptic Christians recorded on a five-minute
video that was released on February 15. Reported-
ly, those martyred were given the opportunity to

renounce Christianity, which they refused to do, knowing that martyrdom awaited them.

This was yet another episode in the bloodiest era of persecution in the history of Christianity. Citing a report by the Roman Catholic Church, *Newsweek* shared, "The report examined the plight of the Christians in China, Egypt, Eritrea, India, Iran, Iraq, Nigeria, North Korea, Pakistan, Saudi Arabia, Sudan, Syria and Turkey over the period lasting 2015 until 2017. The research showed that in that time, Christian suffered crimes against humanity, and some were hanged and crucified. The report found that Saudi Arabia was the only country where the situation for Christians did not get worse, and that was only because the situation couldn't get any worse than it already was."[99]

One of the primary purposes in Peter's writing to the pilgrims that comprised the burgeoning Church was to warn them that they would not necessarily be going from victory to victory, at least in the commonly held view.

There were already dark clouds on the horizon as witnessed by the severe, albeit limited persecution by Emperor Nero. When a fire devastated Rome, thought to be set at Nero's instruction to institute a program of urban renewal, the emperor quickly blamed the misunderstood and largely despised Christians. Believers were hounded and many gathered up for a spectacular persecution. Among the methods employed by Nero included covering Christians in pitch, putting them on a pole, and using them to light his garden at night. He also joyed in putting some in animal skins and turning wild animals on them. It is thought that both Peter and Paul were martyred during Nero's reign. Although the persecution was largely limited to Rome, Peter and others discerned that larger and more severe persecutions would be on the way. They were right.

Jews had been persecuted throughout their history and, though they hated it, it did not come as much of a surprise to them as it would to the Gentile believers. Rome had been tolerant of most religions in the empire but the Christians' refusal to compromise by worshipping the emperor, and their withdrawal from the debauchery considered acceptable to all around them made them targets.

Peter called what was coming a "fiery ordeal." The term chosen was one used for the refining process of gold and silver. This testing takes a person to the essentials, the core of his beliefs. If Christianity is only a social sort of thing or only a religious sentiment, a pretender will flee from paying the cost. But if it is the real deal, the believer will have all pretense, all that is unworthy burned away as the Spirit of God uses the ordeal to purify the believer.

He also warned that this was not going away— that things were likely to get worse. There is a very natural assumption that if someone is living a righteous life, obeys the rules and treats others well, the end result should be that good things will come. While that may hold true for many things, it is not an absolute. In fact, because a person lives righteously for the glory of God, persecution may be inevitable. As Paige Patterson has noted, "The Christian, by virtue of his profession, is on a collision course with suffering."[100]

We all hope trouble will go away or that the pain will subside. But when it is not going away, when things are predicted to get worse, there is a sobering reckoning that must occur. What is important in what Peter is saying is that the suffering to be endured is not because of what comes in the normal course of life. Believers and unbelievers both suffer from reversals in health, mental issues, loss of fortune, prospects, and family woes. That is simply the hard life that all people face.

But what he is talking about is the suffering for Christ's sake. He told them to rejoice, and the Greek tense insists that they are to keep on rejoicing in the face of pain. The reason? "...inasmuch as you participate in the sufferings of Christ" (vs. 13). We cannot participate in the redeeming work of Christ because He alone can atone for sins. But as He was scarred in His suffering, we too, can share in His sufferings, and bear our own scars as a result. With Paul, we can say, "I bear in my body the marks of Jesus" (Galatians 6:17).

There is a promise in the persecution. You will be "overjoyed when His glory is revealed" (vs. 13). This road is going somewhere, this ordeal is more than the result of the wickedness of hateful people. We who suffer for Christ will exchange our personal pains borne for His sake for the glory our Lord will reveal. We remember Joseph's words to his brothers: "You intended to harm me, but God intended it for good to accomplish what is now being done," (Genesis 50:20).

The word "glory" is felt by many commentators to refer to the Shekinah glory that filled the Tabernacle and led the Children of Israel through the Wilderness. Although it may recall that, the immediate application is "that the Spirit bestows His glory on believers. The future 'glory' invades their present experiences of the sanctifying Spirit."[101]

Peter further broadened the definition of suffering beyond the extremes of martyrdom, exile or loss of property. In speaking about bearing insults for the name of Christ (vs. 15) he brought it more into the arena where most of us operate. The insults are not directed toward us because of our physical appearance or our perceived lack of intelligence but specifically because we are followers of Jesus Christ. Nicholson points out, "Contemptuous treatment inflicts greater suffering upon some sensitive souls than physical abuse or the destruction of property."[102]

The question for us in this moment is straightforward: If called upon to suffer for the name of Christ, how will we stand?

## DISCUSSION QUESTIONS:

1. Have you ever suffered for the name of Christ? How did it happen? If not, why were you spared?

2. How shall we explain to a new believer that he/she may have to suffer for Christ's sake?

3. Given the current state of affairs in our world, what is the likelihood of persecution increasing toward the Christian faith and toward you as a Christian in particular?

# 26

# JUDGMENT

*If you suffer, it should not be as a murderer or thief or any other kind of criminal, or even as a meddler. However, if you suffer as a Christian, do not be ashamed, but praise God that you bear that name. For it is time for judgment to begin with God's household; and if it begins with us, what will the outcome be for those who do not obey the gospel of God? And,*

*"If it is hard for the righteous to be saved, what will become of the ungodly and the sinner?"*

*So then, those who suffer according to God's will should commit themselves to their*

*faithful Creator and continue to do good.*
1 Peter 4:15-19

Fiorello LaGuardia, who served as mayor of New York City from 1933 to 1945, began his career as a judge. One day, a poor old man was brought before him, charged with stealing a loaf of bread. "I've got to punish you," LaGuardia said, "Because there is no exception to the law. I can do nothing but sentence you to a fine of $10."

LaGuardia reached into his pocket, saying, "Here's the $10 to pay the fine. Now I remit the fine. Furthermore, I'm going to fine everybody in this courtroom 50 cents for living in a town where a man has to steal bread in order to eat. Mr. Bailiff, collect the fines and give them to his man." The man walked out with $47.50, a hefty amount in those days.[103]

As Peter continued to address believers during the trying days in which they lived and having warned them about sins in relationships, he now turned to crimes against society. While some of these are extreme, Peter knew that Christianity represented something that was strongly countercultural. Movements that go against the established way of doing things often become militant, and doing so, they can be given to excesses. The French Revolution started as a correction to the abuses of the aristocracy in France but without restraints, it degenerated into the infamous Reign of Terror. Unchecked fanaticism can be dressed in Christian clothing, but it is evil just the same.

Murder included the practice of exposing unwanted or defective babies to the elements so they would die, a common practice among non-Jews in biblical times. We are to have a reverence for life, including that of the unborn and those who might be deemed a burden to society.[104] Euthanasia is equally an afront to God. Artificially prolonging a life when there is no hope of healing presents another scenario. We must be careful about serving our own needs and those who would otherwise pass from this life. That is quite different from engineering death by taking action to end it.

Nor are we allowed to become a thief or be involved in any other criminal activity. Being a Christian was enough of an offense to garner punishment, but if believers are involved in any kind of crime, we compromise our witness. If someone professes to be a Christian but is engaged in criminal activity, the charge of hypocrisy is not an insult but an earned accusation. Kenyon is quoted as saying, "A 'sinning religion' is a projection of paganism in the guise of piousness."[105]

It is interesting that, in the list of crimes, Peter talked about meddling. The work of a busybody was as deeply offensive in the Greco-Roman and the Jewish cultures as it is today. The turning of affections and sowing of discord based as much on half-truths, outright deception, or a lack of discretion has destroyed too many families and friendships. But there is another definition that means "one who claims an authority, like that of a bishop or superintendent in a region in which he has no right to exercise it."[106] We now call that a boundary issue.

On the other hand, suffering as a Christian causes us not to be ashamed but to praise God. We are reminded of the apostles, who after healing many were brought up on charges by the Sanhedrin, beaten, and told not to do anything else in the name of Jesus. "The apostles left the Sanhedrin, rejoicing because they had been counted worthy of suffering disgrace for the Name" (Acts 5:41). Circulating a few years ago was the question, "If you were arrested for being a Christian, would there be enough evidence to convict you?" Peter is simply saying that if they were accused of any crime it should only be as a follower of Jesus Christ.

A sobering reminder about judgment is next. "For it is time to begin with God's household; and if it begins with us, what will the outcome be for those who do not obey the gospel?" (vs. 17). As in our opening illustration, we are absolutely guilty of the sins and crimes we have committed in violation of God's law. But through Christ, the penalty has been paid resulting not only in our freedom but with God heaping blessing upon blessing over and above our need. The judgment that begins in the house of God flows from the cross where our sins were forgiven, and we passed into a new life.

God continues to work in us to make us into the holy beings we were meant to be. The ongoing judgment of God is in His holding us accountable for how we live our lives, what we do with the gifts and opportunities He gives us, and how we work to expand His kingdom. In order to do so, from time to time God must break our hearts, just as a physician has to break bones at times so that they can heal properly. Witherington points out, "They are disciplined now so they will not have to face the final judgment later…Christians are not being punished in the fiery ordeal; they are being tested and purified."[107]

If there is pain for the believer as God purifies him, what will be the impact on the unbeliever? Some of the judgment is already operating in our world because many sins have punishments already built in. Those who are sexually immoral run the risk of venereal disease; the thief will likely end up in jail. There is no delay in judgment being passed. But many sins remain undiscovered at least to human eyes. God is not fooled. The unforgiven sinner is accountable for all the deeds he has done.

Throughout his letter, Peter reminded the believers that this is not the only stage on which the drama is being played. Right now, things are happening; but then there is eternity, the coming again of Christ to establish His kingdom. There will be a judgment then, and if Christians have had to work through issues, what of those who have not taken their soul's salvation seriously at all? They are defenseless, without a word that can be whispered in their defense for having disregarded Christ. They will know in that awful moment that their sins condemn them to a deserved punishment that is in place because of their refusal to yield their lives to Christ. Salvation Army author Elizabeth Swift Brengle wrote bluntly, "If you go to Hell, it will be over the mangled body of Jesus."[108]

"Those who suffer according to God's will should commit themselves to their faithful Creator and continue to do good" (vs. 19). Barclay shares the word "commit is a technical word for depositing money with a trusted friend."[109] In reminding them that they are entrusting themselves to the Creator, it calls to mind that He who set the stars in motion and whose laws unfailingly keep order is the one who is looking out for them. Our response is to continue to do good as He has done good for us.

## DISCUSSION QUESTIONS

1. When has meddling been a problem in your life?

2. Why is God's discipline important in the life of the believer?

3. How do you feel about the plight of the unbeliever?

# 27

# A WORD TO THE ELDERS

*To the elders among you, I appeal as a fellow elder and a witness of Christ's sufferings who also will share in the glory to be revealed: Be shepherds of God's flock that is under your care, watching over them—not because you must, but because you are willing, as God wants you to be; not pursuing dishonest gain, but eager to serve; not lording it over those entrusted to you, but being examples to the flock. And when the Chief Shepherd appears, you will receive the crown of glory that will never fade away.* 1 Peter 5:1-4

The legendary NFL Hall of Fame coach of the Miami Dolphins for many years, Don Shula, spoke about the power of example:

> During the 1994-1995 season, I had what I thought was a calcium spur on my heel. It became so painful to move around on the practice field every day that I began to wear something like a ski boot at practice to reduce some of the pain. I didn't want to take time to correct the problem until after the season. I can't ask my players to play hurt if I wimp out when I'm hurting a little bit. Finally, I had no choice. One day in early December, when I was heading off the field after a practice, I felt something pop. It turned out I'd ruptured my Achilles tendon…The day I had the operation was the first regular-season practice I had missed in my twenty-five years with the Dolphins.

Shula was back the next day, getting around on a golf cart. He led by example.[110]

For Peter, there were other important matters besides persecution against believers. They still had to maintain the mechanics of organization in the burgeoning church. While we may be excited about the dramatic movements of the Spirit, without organization and structure, many of the gains can be lost. Even those who rebel against the established order find that they must at some point establish a structure, which oftentimes is remarkably similar to the one from which they rebelled.

The Bible does not come out plainly and say, "This is how a church is to be set up." Not surprisingly, the early church took the structure of the synagogue and brought it over.[111] No doubt some synagogues became Christian, maintaining their structure in the process. Because of Roman persecution, the church could not be highly centralized, although the apostles had authority over doctrinal and disciplinary matters. When Christianity was made the official religion of the empire by Constantine, the church hierarchy mirrored the organization of the Roman Empire which had proved to be a highly efficient form of government.

At this stage of the church's development, the role of the elders was important, who were so named because most of them were older. In addressing them, Peter identified himself as an elder himself, not an apostle, for a humbler and gentler approach. He reminded them that he was a witness to Christ's suffering. At first, this seems strange because he was one of the disciples who fled when Jesus was arrested. Later, he denied Christ, and from the Gospel record, only John was actually at the cross. But as Witherington points out, "It does not necessarily imply eyewitness, but one who witnesses about something."[112]

Peter told them, "Be shepherds of God's flock under your care, watching over them" (vs. 2). The image of shepherd was often used in the Old Testament for spiritual leaders. Peter vividly remembered that crucial conversation he had with Jesus following the resurrection when Jesus instructed him to "Feed My lambs," "Take care of My sheep," and "Feed My sheep" (John 21:15-17). Paralleling the duties of an earthly shepherd toward their flock, he was to feed, lead, guide, guard, and bring them to safety. But as he was reminded, the flock is not his—it belongs to God.

There are temptations that are faced by anyone in a leadership position but especially those in ministry. Peter told them to watch over the flock "not because you must, but because you are willing" (vs. 2). It is a high privilege to lead the people of God. Working halfheartedly will not do, nor with a feeling of being under obligation by family or others' expectations. God wants our loving service, not our complaining compliance.

"Not pursuing dishonest gain" (vs. 2). Greed is one of the major sins of ministry. It is strange that those who have professed to set their hearts on heaven are so tempted to feather their nest on earth. Greed is present in all people—just stick your head into any preschool class to see it in action. Those in ministry should have their needs provided, of course. But it is coveting the something more, like the other guy has, that transforms a shepherd into a hireling. It is not only the materialism that is a problem but the degeneration of mindset from seeing people as sheep to be fed to commodities to be exploited.

Peter warned of another temptation: "Not lording it over those entrusted to you" (vs. 3). The abuse of power is one of the gravest sins of clergy and those in church leadership. It can be seen in the promotion of self, taking advantage of position for personal gain, mistreatment, or outright exploitation of those under their care. The idea that sinful liberties are entitlements undercuts the spiritual standing and authority of leaders. "Believers are to have one Lord; they do not need another."[113]

Instead, we are to be "eager to serve...examples to the flock" (vs. 2, 3). Service humbly given in the

Lord's name to His people is a powerful example of leadership as God intended. As God loves His people, we are to love them, sacrificially, unselfishly. "If the people see the pastor as a ruler, the pastor must see himself as a servant."[114]

The final verse in this section reminds, "And when the Chief Shepherd appears, you will receive the crown of glory that will never fade away" (vs. 4). Here is a call to accountability, a promise of care, and a reward that is to be ours. As shepherds, we are accountable to the Chief Shepherd. That is why leadership must be taken up with serious thought, pursued with all effort, and lived without reproach.

As the Chief Shepherd, once again we are reminded of His tender care for His people. Those in leadership, while tending to the needs of others, have needs of their own. They are not spared from life's uncertainties, its disappointments, or its problems. We need the Chief Shepherd to bind our wounds and lead us to safe pasture.

Peter uses a familiar figure when speaking of the reward awaiting the faithful. "Here is the image of a crown of unfading flowers (amaranths are in view, considered especially durable; and their red color did not quickly fade), such as was presented to those who won an event in the Greek games."[115] We have all seen the athlete in the moment of victory. There is great joy as she celebrates the crowning moment. And for you who cares for the flock of God there will be that kind of celebration when the Chief Shepherd crowns you with your reward, whether that be leadership of a Sunday school class with nursery babies or a congregation in the thousands.

## DISCUSSION QUESTIONS

1. Why is organization and structure important in the church?

2. How can a leader guard against the temptations that compromise ministry?

3. Think of the moment you receive your reward from the Lord. What will that be like?

## 28

# A WORD TO THE YOUNGERS

*In the same way, you who are younger,
submit yourselves to your elders. All
of you, clothe yourselves with humility
toward one another, because,*

*"God opposes the proud
but shows favor to the humble."*

*Humble yourselves, therefore, under God's
mighty hand, that He may lift you up in
due time. Cast all your anxiety on Him
because He cares for you.* 1 Peter 5:5-7

Canute, a Danish king who sat on the throne of England in the twelfth century, was weary of the flattery and extravagant praise of his power, greatness, and invincibility. He ordered that his throne be taken to the seashore. He commanded the waves not to come in and wet him. Soaked from the tides that ignored his commands, he returned to his palace where he took his crown and hung it on a statue of the crucified Christ, never to wear it again.[116]

Having addressed the elders, Peter now spoke to the younger leaders in the congregation. They were told, "submit to your elders. All of you clothe yourselves with humility toward one another" (vs. 5).

The young tend to be impatient, change-oriented, and activists. Their energy and vision inspire others to get involved, shake off the doldrums, and get things done. The church is tremendously benefitted by the younger ones and relies heavily on them to get things accomplished. The biggest problem we have regarding the young leaders is that there are not enough of them.

In order for all to work properly, there has to be a partnership between the younger members and the older ones. The older ones can share what they have learned. There is absolutely no substitute for experience. Many of us who are older wish there was. It would be nice to be able to learn all we needed to know by being directed to the right book. But many of the most valuable lessons can only come via skinned knees and bruises. Fortunately, we can learn some things by listening to the stories of others. Life is difficult enough without making it more so by not listening.

Peter called on all to "clothe yourselves with humility" (vs. 5). The reference to "clothe" is one of contrasts. It can refer to a long stole-like robe that was a sign of honor and importance.[117] It can also refer to an apron worn by slaves that they bound up around themselves to keep from getting dirty while they worked.[118] Barclay comments, "We, too, in all things put on the apron of humility in the service of Christ and our fellowmen; but that very apron of humility will become the garment of honor for us, for it is he who is the servant of all who is greatest in the Kingdom of Heaven."[119]

Humility is not the downing of oneself nor is it equal to having an inferiority complex. It is not being insipid, blending into the woodwork to avoid being noticed. The humble person has a true estimate of himself in the sight of God. As previously discussed by Peter (4:10-12), we are to exercise our gifts for God's glory; but if we are afraid to speak up and put them into use, it is not humility we exercise but a form of selfishness, similar to the evil servant who buried his talent rather than putting it to use for his master (Matthew 25:14-30).

A baseball player knows he has done well by hitting a homerun—the evidence is there without him saying anything. And the child of God can know by the evidence that his efforts produced if he has accomplished something good. The issue is pride versus humility in those moments. A humble person will rejoice that there was the right outcome, whereas the proud will seek recognition and a better place for himself because of his superior efforts. When we know who we are in Christ, we acknowledge our gifts, our talents, our limitations, and our humanity as a flawed being. The true inventory of who and what we are is enough to keep us humble. We can always take a lower position because we know we are not diminished by any task and nothing is below us.

Peter warned that "God opposes the proud" (vs.5). The idea is that God sets Himself in battle array against any who would be prideful.[120] The proud person does not prove that he has bested another or stands superior. Rather, he has committed an act of war against the Almighty God. The odds are not in his favor.

"Humble yourselves…under God's mighty hand" (vs. 6) is a call to immediate action.[121] The urgency reveals that unless humility is in place, God cannot work through an individual as He would, nor can that person become all that God intends for him to be.

Humility is conditional to the promise, "that He may lift you up in due time" (vs. 6). God has a destiny for each one of His children. When we accept Him in salvation, He begins a work in us with our cooperation. If we seek to be holy as He is holy, we begin to see things happening that we could not have imagined. The act of lifting us up is not necessarily in the eyes of the people around us, although that might happen. It is God molding us into what we could never have become without Him at work in our lives. We humbly lay our lives before Him and watch Him begin to work. "In due time" reminds us that God has His own timetable for us, which we are wise neither to rush nor to delay.

"Cast all your anxiety on Him, because He cares for you" (vs. 7). A favorite verse for many, this verse invites us to gather all the fears and misgivings, the cares and concerns, and throw them on His back. Those memories that haunt, the words that still cut after all this time, those troubling thoughts that rob us of our sleep, the times we have been overlooked or forgotten, our hurts and sorrows were never meant to be borne by us alone. If we could have gotten rid of them ourselves, we would have; but too often we find they remain. Cast them on Him. When you throw a dirty shirt in the laundry you don't hold onto it through the wash cycle. You have to let go to get it clean. Let go. Trust. For He cares for you.

## DISCUSSION QUESTIONS

1. In what ways can we aid younger members in their service to Christ? If you are younger, what do you wish the older people you work with understood?

2. What care do you need to cast on the Lord?

3. What does it mean to you that by humbling yourself God will lift you up?

# 29

# PROWLING LION

*Be alert and of sober mind. Your enemy the devil prowls around like a roaring lion looking for someone to devour. Resist him, standing firm in the faith, because you know that the family of believers throughout the world is undergoing the same kind of sufferings.*

*And the God of all grace, who called you to His eternal glory in Christ, after you have suffered a little while, will Himself restore you and make you strong, firm and steadfast. To Him be the power for ever and ever. Amen.* 1 Peter 5:8-11

Tony Evans tells the story of a schoolboy who was constantly beaten up by a bully. One day on his way to school, the bully pounced on the boy once again. But this time, the little guy said, "Come on. I'll take you right now." Angry, the bully moved toward him. It was then that the little boy's 6' 10", 275-pound father stepped out of the bushes. The bully could do nothing else but whisper, "Oh, no."[122]

Peter warned the believers that they, too, had to face a bully. "Be alert and of sober mind. Your enemy, the devil prowls around like a roaring lion looking for someone to devour" (vs. 8). While there may be some who dismiss the idea of the devil, the Bible takes his existence very seriously.

Peter told the believers to "be alert," which is a military metaphor, calling for decisive action.[123] The ancient city of Sardis, once the wealthiest in the world, was built on a high precipice with formidable walls. In spite of this, it was conquered not once, but twice. When the Persians came to attack, they could not breach its defenses. But the clay used for the walls tended to crumble and crack. One night, a soldier on watch dropped his helmet. The Persians surrounding the city watched as the soldier came to the base of the wall to retrieve it. They surmised that there was another way to enter the city that the soldier used. The next night when the guards had fallen asleep, a small band of Persians found the crack in the wall, opened the gates and the city fell.[124] We face a similar defeat at Satan's hands if we fail to be alert.

The term for "enemy" was a term used for a legal adversary in a lawsuit.[125] It has that same meaning in Job. From the picture drawn of him there, we learn that Satan intelligently plans his attack on the faithful. It is warfare in its truest sense.

Peter said he is like a prowling, roaring lion. In Satan's prowling and roaring he is always hungry, always seeking prey. Now nearly extinct, Peter was referring to the Asiatic lion, slightly smaller than the more familiar African lion but every bit as aggressive. Lions stilled roamed freely throughout the Middle East, often attacking along roadways or even within villages. The person who failed to maintain his guard could well find himself a victim. Christians of this time would be well aware that lions were now part of the games in the Coliseum and other venues. Some of those who heard Peter's words being read in their churches would have such a lion as one of the last sights as they were martyred in the persecutions. The word "devour" in Greek literally means, "drink down," meaning that there would be no trace left.[126]

The answer is to "resist him...standing firm" (vs. 9). In spite of his power, he is not unconquerable. The constant reminders by Peter throughout his letter about the power of God in salvation, over death, and His ultimate reign over all puts Satan in perspective. In the power of the Spirit, Satan can be defeated, utterly and completely. Hilary of Arles said, "There is a world of difference between God and the devil. If you resist God, He will destroy you, but if you resist the devil, you will destroy him."[127]

They were not facing this alone. Not only did they have the promise of the Lord caring for and shepherding them, but they stood shoulder to shoulder with other believers who were also undergoing suffering. As a fellow cancer survivor, when I hear someone who has cancer or has survived cancer, I feel a tug deep in my heart. I remember the long, difficult days of chemotherapy, the total weakness, the uncertainty of whether or not I would survive the ordeal. Suffering forms a kinship with others going through the same thing. Although there is verbal support, or the warmth of an understanding hug, much of the comfort comes in knowing that someone else has travelled that same road. In a deeper way, there is a fellowship of suffering for those who have been tried for the sake of Christ.

After the grim discussion of Satan and suffering, Peter closed this section with affirmation. "To God alone belongs eternal might, which makes Roman glory look like a withered flower."[128]

Peter had listed sins that bedeviled believers. Now he lists four things that God was doing on their behalf.

**Restore**. The idea is making everything fit together into a complete object or setting right what had been wrong. It was the term used for mending nets or healing broken bones.[129]

**Strong**. There were so many times they felt powerless and weak. But Peter told them they were being made strong, a word that means "to fix, to make firm or solid" and was used when buttressing a wall.[130]

**Firm**. To strengthen, make strong.

**Steadfast**. The term was used for establishing foundations upon which the buildings were built.[131] The foundations often remain hidden but were essential. So, the believer will find that much of their strength is internal, unseen perhaps on the outside but solid fortitude within.

## DISCUSSION QUESTIONS

1. How is Satan at work today?

2. How are we strengthened by shared suffering?

3. Describe a time when God strengthened you. What did you learn from it?

# 30

# LOVE AND PEACE

*With the help of Silas, whom I regard as a
faithful brother, I have written to you briefly,
encouraging you and testifying that this is
the true grace of God. Stand fast in it.*

*She who is in Babylon, chosen together with
you, sends you her greetings, and so does my
son Mark. Greet one another with a kiss of love.*

*Peace to all of you who are in Christ.*
1 Peter 5:12-14

.

As was the custom for letters in this day, Peter closed his with some final remarks of farewell as well as acknowledgments.

From what we understand, he wrote this while in prison in Rome, which terminated with his execution. Prisons in that day were not at all like today. They were used almost exclusively as a holding place until someone's execution. Because of that, prisoners received only the most meager meals, disease was rampant, filth prevailed, and ventilation was close to non-existent. The miserable conditions were meant to further punish the condemned. If there was any relief it was because the prisoner had visitors who might bring in some food and medicine. But when they did, they had to endure the stench and conditions of the jail. Peter had such a friend.

Peter thanked Silvanus for his help. Silvanus was almost certainly also known as Silas, the traveling companion of Paul in the book of Acts. Although we do not know the full extent of his relationship with Peter or his responsibilities, essentially, he fulfilled one or a combination of the following functions:

1. He carried the letter to the churches.

2. He was an amanuensis, a kind of executive secretary, to whom Peter dictated this letter. Some have suggested that in this role he may have helped Peter with the Greek, since a high quality of Greek is used in the letter. It is assumed as a fisherman and as a leader in the church he would not have had the opportunity to master the language to the degree it appears in First Peter.

3. Silas actually wrote the letter under Peter's direction. This would mean it was still Peter's thoughts as inspired by the Holy Spirit but that the words, order, and presentation were done by Silas.[132]

Silas was far more than clerical help. Peter had high confidence in him, and they likely enjoyed a strong friendship. Many of us are fortunate to have brothers or sisters in the faith with whom we share a deep bond, made stronger because of our allegiance to the same Lord. Often this is their spouse. For others, the close relationship with a spouse is supplemented by such a friend, one that Proverbs says, "There is a friend who sticks closer than a brother"

(18:24b). I have been blessed with such a friend for over forty years. Over that time, we have enjoyed countless laughs, shared our heartbreaks, counseled, challenged, reproved, and listened to each other when counsel or listening was most needed. I have a wonderful wife but also enjoy the rich fellowship of Frank, my best friend. I am always a little sad when I hear someone say that they have no close friend given the benefits my own soul and heart have gleaned from this friendship.

Silas was likely that for Peter. He disregarded the filth and stench of the prison to be with him, to serve with him as Peter shared what was perhaps this one last act of ministry in writing the letter. We don't hear a lot about Silas, but because Paul and Peter both have their names linked with his, we can say that he knew what it was to be a friend of someone who outshone him, and he didn't care that they did. Someone has said that the hardest instrument to play is second fiddle. Silas was a virtuoso second fiddle.

The whole theme of his letter is found in two words: stand fast (vs. 12). Sometimes standing fast is all we can do. We can't advance. Retreat is unthinkable. But we can hold the ground that we have taken. We can be faithful when we can simply do nothing else. Since so many fail at this point, it is not the least we can do but is often the best we can do.

In a cryptic sign-off, Peter sent a greeting from the church in Babylon. By this time, the once mighty city of Babylon was nothing more than a tiny village on the edge of its ruins. There was also a Babylon in Egypt, but it was remote and obscure. From Revelation we know that Babylon was the code word for Rome. It is extremely likely that it is this way that Peter used it. Known for its wealth and decadence, the great city of Babylon made the nations tremble in its glory. It was Babylon that carried the inhabitants of Judah away following the war against it. And it was from Babylon that the Jews were freed to return to Jerusalem where they rebuilt the Temple and the city.

The Jews were captives in Babylon, strangers and exiles. The Christians were strangers and exiles under the thumb of Rome. The God who had delivered the Jews from Babylon would deliver the believers from the hand of Rome.

With that assurance, Peter could close, "Peace to all of you who are in Christ."

## DISCUSSION QUESTIONS

1. How is friendship strengthened when both are committed followers of Christ?

2. In what ways does a Christian stand fast?

3. How are believers strangers and exiles?

# ENDNOTES

**Devotion 1**

1. Ben Witherington III, *Letters and Homilies for Hellenized Christians, Vol. II* (Downer's Grove, IL: Inter-Varsity Press, 2007), 69

2. "Eugene Lang, Investor Who Made College Dreams a Reality, Dies at 98" https://www.nytimes.com/2017/04/08/nyregion/eugene-lang-dead-harlem-college.html Accessed 10/16/19

3. Ben Witherington III, *Letters and Homilies for Hellenized Christians, Vol. II* (Downer's Grove, IL: Inter-Varsity Press, 2007), 79

**Devotion 2**

4. Bray, Gerald, Editor, *Ancient Christian Commentary on Scripture Vol. XI* (Downer's Grove, IL: Inter-Varsity Press, 2000), 70

5. Jobes, Karen H. *1 Peter* (Grand Rapids, IL: Baker Academic, 2005), 85

**Devotion 3**

6. "Metallurgy" *The International Standard Bible Encyclopedia*. https://www.bible-history.com/isbe/m/metallurgy/ Accessed October 16, 2019

7. D. Edmund Hiebert, *1 Peter* (Winona Lake, IL: BMH Books, 1992), 65

8. Charles S. Ball, *The Wesleyan Bible Commentary Vol. VI* (Grand Rapids, MI: Baker Book House, 1966), 252

9. Bray, Gerald, Editor, *Ancient Christian Commentary on Scripture Vol. XI* (Downer's Grove, IL: Inter-Varsity Press, 2000), 72

**Devotion 4**
10. Ker Than, "Scientists Unlock Mystery of Ancient Greek Machine" Live Science https://www.livescience.com/1166-scientists-unravel-mystery-ancient-greek-machine.html Accessed October 16, 2019
11. Ben Witherington III, *Letters and Homilies for Hellenized Christians, Vol. II* (Downer's Grove, IL: Inter-Varsity Press, 2007), 83
12. Paige Patterson, *A Pilgrim Priesthood* (Eugene, OR: Wipf & Stock Publishers, 2004), 46
13. *The Song Book of The Salvation Army* #241 (Alexandria, VA: The Salvation Army, 20116

**Devotion 5**
14. Allen Satterlee, *Notable Quotables: A Compendium of Gems from Salvation Army Literature* (Atlanta: The Salvation Army), 93
15. Daniel G. Powers, *1 & 2 Peter, Jude: a Commentary in the Wesleyan Tradition* (Kansas City, MO: Beacon Hill Press, 2010), 69
16. Ben Witherington III, *Letters and Homilies for Hellenized Christians, Vol. II* (Downer's Grove, IL: Inter-Varsity Press, 2007), 97

**Devotion 6**
None

**Devotion 7**
17. Allen Satterlee, *Determined to Conquer: The History of The Salvation Army in the Caribbean* (Alexandria, VA: Crest Books, 2012), 62
18. D. Edmund Hiebert, *1 Peter* (Winona Lake, IL: BMH Books, 1992), 113
19. Ibid., 113

**Devotion 8**
20. Rachel Kaufman, "32,000-Year-Old Plant Brought Back to Life – Oldest Yet" https://www.nationalgeographic.com/news/2012/2/120221-oldest-seeds-regenerated-plants-science/ Accessed October 17, 2019
21. David A. Case & David W. Holdren, *1-2 Peter, 1-3 John, Jude: A Commentary for Bible Students* (Indianapolis, IN: Wesleyan Publishing House, 2005), 51
22. "An Inspiring Introduction to the Holy Book" http://blog.gideons.org/2010/12/the-bible-contains-the-mind-of-god/ Accessed October 17, 2019

**Devotion 9**
23. Lisa Capretto, "The Health Benefits of Milk" http://www.oprah.com/food/the-health-benefits-of-milk/all Accessed October 17, 2019
24. Jobes, Karen H. *1 Peter* (Grand Rapids, IL: Baker Academic, 2005), 131
25. Ben Witherington III, *Letters and Homilies for Hellenized Christians, Vol. II* (Downer's Grove, IL: Inter-Varsity Press, 2007), 111
26. Roy S. Nicholson, *Beacon Bible Commentary, Hebrews-Revelation Vol. 10* (Kansas City, MO: Beacon Hill Press, 1967), 278

27. D. Edmund Hiebert, *1 Peter* (Winona Lake, IL: BMH Books, 1992), 126

## Devotion 10
None

## Devotion 11
28. Bray, Gerald, Editor, *Ancient Christian Commentary on Scripture Vol. XI* (Downer's Grove, IL: Inter-Varsity Press, 2000), 87
29. *Wesley Bible Studies* (Indianapolis, IN: Wesleyan Publishing House, 2014), 32

## Devotion 12
30. Jobes, Karen H. *1 Peter* (Grand Rapids, IL: Baker Academic, 2005), 170
31. D. Edmund Hiebert, *1 Peter* (Winona Lake, IL: BMH Books, 1992), 156
32. William Barclay, *The Letters of James and Peter* (Philadelphia: The Westminster Press, 1960), 239
33. Paige Patterson, *A Pilgrim Priesthood* (Eugene, OR: Wipf & Stock Publishers, 2004), 87
34. Allen Satterlee, *Notable Quotables: a Compendium of Gems from Salvation Army Literature* (Atlanta: The Salvation Army), 237
35. Ben Witherington III, *Letters and Homilies for Hellenized Christians, Vol. II* (Downer's Grove, IL: Inter-Varsity Press, 2007), 145

**Devotion 13**

36. Mark Cartwright, "Slavery in the Roman World" Ancient History Encyclopedia https://www.ancient.eu/article/629/slavery-in-the-roman-world/ Accessed October 17, 2019

37. William Barclay, *The Letters of James and Peter* (Philadelphia: The Westminster Press, 1960), 250

38. Jobes, Karen H. *1 Peter* (Grand Rapids, IL: Baker Academic, 2005), 185

39. aige Patterson, *A Pilgrim Priesthood* (Eugene, OR: Wipf & Stock Publishers, 2004), 95

40. William Barclay, *The Letters of James and Peter* (Philadelphia: The Westminster Press, 1960), 251, 252

41. D. Edmund Hiebert, *1 Peter* (Winona Lake, IL: BMH Books, 1992), 178

**Devotion 14**

42. Ben Witherington III, *Letters and Homilies for Hellenized Christians, Vol. II* (Downer's Grove, IL: Inter-Varsity Press, 2007), 155

43. D. Edmund Hiebert, *1 Peter* (Winona Lake, IL: BMH Books, 1992), 183

**Devotion 15**

44. Mark. W. Merrill, "Five Things Husbands Wish Their Wives Knew" http://www.markmerrill.com/5-things-husbands-wish-wives-knew/?__hstc=123427924.a3e3ef254b2846b61389b4292d7d4d6f.1571427027157.1571427027157.1571427027157.1&__hssc=123427924.4.1571427027157&__hsfp=2973072507 Accessed October 17, 2019

45. William Barclay, *The Letters of James and Peter* (Philadelphia: The Westminster Press, 1960), 259

46. Ibid., 264-265

47. Jobes, Karen H. *1 Peter* (Grand Rapids, IL: Baker Academic, 2005), 203

48. Edmund Hiebert, *1 Peter* (Winona Lake, IL: BMH Books, 1992), 195

49. Jobes, Karen H. *1 Peter* (Grand Rapids, IL: Baker Academic, 2005), 203

50. David A. Case & David W. Holdren, *1-2 Peter, 1-3 John, Jude: A Commentary for Bible Students* (Indianapolis, IN: Wesleyan Publishing House, 2005), 88

51. William Barclay, *The Letters of James and Peter* (Philadelphia: The Westminster Press, 1960), 260

**Devotion 16**

52. Mark W. Merrill, "What Wives Wish Their Husbands Understood". https://www.allprodad.com/5-things-wives-wish-husbands-knew/ Accessed October 17, 2019

53. David A. Case & David W. Holdren, *1-2 Peter, 1-3 John, Jude: A Commentary for Bible Students* (Indianapolis, IN: Wesleyan Publishing House, 2005), 90

54. Ben Witherington III, *Letters and Homilies for Hellenized Christians, Vol. II* (Downer's Grove, IL: Inter-Varsity Press, 2007), 167

55. Bray, Gerald, Editor, *Ancient Christian Commentary on Scripture Vol. XI* (Downer's Grove, IL: Inter-Varsity Press, 2000), 99

56. Daniel G. Powers, *1 & 2 Peter, Jude: a Commentary in the Wesleyan Tradition* (Kansas City, MO: Beacon Hill Press, 2010), 111

## Devotion 17

57. Monk Preston, "The Monk Who Ended the Coliseum Games" http://www.prayerfoundation.org/favoritemonks/favorite_monks_telemachus_coliseum.htm Accessed October 19, 2019

58. D. Edmund Hiebert, *1 Peter* (Winona Lake, IL: BMH Books, 1992), 212

59. William Barclay, *The Letters of James and Peter* (Philadelphia: The Westminster Press, 1960), 268

60. D. Edmund Hiebert, *1 Peter* (Winona Lake, IL: BMH Books, 1992), 213

61. Ben Witherington III, *Letters and Homilies for Hellenized Christians, Vol. II* (Downer's Grove, IL: Inter-Varsity Press, 2007), 168-169

62. Jobes, Karen H. *1 Peter* (Grand Rapids, IL: Baker Academic, 2005), 218

## Devotion 18

63. "Hubble Space Telescope Facts" https://www.nasa.gov/mission_pages/hubble/story/index.html Accessed October 19, 2019

64. Paige Patterson, *A Pilgrim Priesthood* (Eugene, OR: Wipf & Stock Publishers, 2004), 120

65. D. Edmund Hiebert, *1 Peter* (Winona Lake, IL: BMH Books, 1992), 216

66. "13 Inspiring Quotes on Doing Good" https://caringmagazine.org/13-inspiring-quotes-on-doing-good/ Accessed October 19, 2019

67. Paige Patterson, *A Pilgrim Priesthood* (Eugene, OR: Wipf & Stock Publishers, 2004), 121

## Devotion 19

68. Richard Collier, *The General Next to God* (New York: E.P. Dutton & Co., 1965), 99

69. Paige Patterson, *A Pilgrim Priesthood* (Eugene, OR: Wipf & Stock Publishers, 2004), 123

70. D. Edmund Hiebert, *1 Peter* (Winona Lake, IL: BMH Books, 1992), 225

71. Paige Patterson, *A Pilgrim Priesthood* (Eugene, OR: Wipf & Stock Publishers, 2004), 123

72. Ben Witherington III, *Letters and Homilies for Hellenized Christians, Vol. II* (Downer's Grove, IL: Inter-Varsity Press, 2007), 179

73. D. Edmund Hiebert, *1 Peter* (Winona Lake, IL: BMH Books, 1992), 227

74. Jobes, Karen H. *1 Peter* (Grand Rapids, IL: Baker Academic, 2005), 232

75. Ibid. 231

## Devotion 20

76. Eleanor Blau, "Declaration of Independence Sells for $2.4 Million". NY Times, June 14, 1991. https://www.nytimes.com/1991/06/14/arts/declaration-of-independence-sells-for-2.4-million.html Accessed October 19, 2019

77. *The Song Book of The Salvation Army*, #208 (Alexandria, VA: The Salvation Army, 2016)

## Devotion 21

78. Roy S. Nicholson, *Beacon Bible Commentary, Hebrews-Revelation Vol. 10* (Kansas City, MO: Beacon Hill Press, 1967), 291

**Devotion 22**

79. H. A. Ironside, *Illustrations of Biblical Truth* (Chicago: Moody Press, 1945), 29-31

80. William Barclay, *The Letters of James and Peter* (Philadelphia: The Westminster Press, 1960), 291

81. D. Edmund Hiebert, *1 Peter* (Winona Lake, IL: BMH Books, 1992), 260

82. Ibid.

83. William Smith, "Bacchanalia", http://penelope. uchicago.edu/Thayer/E/Roman/Texts/secondary/SMIGRA*/ Bacchanalia.html Accessed October 19, 2019

84. D. Edmund Hiebert, *1 Peter* (Winona Lake, IL: BMH Books, 1992), 261

85. Ben Witherington III, *Letters and Homilies for Hellenized Christians, Vol. II* (Downer's Grove, IL: Inter-Varsity Press, 2007), 196

**Devotion 23**

86. Paige Patterson, *A Pilgrim Priesthood* (Eugene, OR: Wipf & Stock Publishers, 2004), 153

87. Walter A. Ewell, Editor. *The Evangelical Dictionary of Theology, Second Edition* (Grand Rapids, MI: Baker Academic, 2001), 639

88. Jobes, Karen H. *1 Peter* (Grand Rapids, IL: Baker Academic, 2005), 270

**Devotion 24**

89. D. Edmund Hiebert, *1 Peter* (Winona Lake, IL: BMH Books, 1992), 270

90. Jobes, Karen H. *1 Peter* (Grand Rapids, IL: Baker Academic, 2005), 277

91. Michael P. Green, *1500 Illustrations for Biblical Preaching* (Grand Rapids, MI: Baker Book House, 1998), 433

92. D. Edmund Hiebert, 1 Peter (Winona Lake, IL: BMH Books, 1992), 271-272

93. Roy S. Nicholson, *Beacon Bible Commentary, Hebrews-Revelation Vol. 10* (Kansas City, MO: Beacon Hill Press, 1967), 295

94. Jobes, Karen H. *1 Peter* (Grand Rapids, IL: Baker Academic, 2005), 280

95. D. Edmund Hiebert, *1 Peter* (Winona Lake, IL: BMH Books, 1992), 275

96. Daniel G. Powers, *1 & 2 Peter, Jude: a Commentary in the Wesleyan Tradition* (Kansas City, MO: Beacon Hill Press, 2010), 134

97. Paige Patterson, *A Pilgrim Priesthood* (Eugene, OR: Wipf & Stock Publishers, 2004), 159

98. Bray, Gerald, Editor, *Ancient Christian Commentary on Scripture Vol. XI* (Downer's Grove, IL: Inter-Varsity Press, 2000), 117

## Devotion 25

99. Christina Maza. As found in https://www.newsweek.com/christian-persecution-genocide-worse-ever-770462. Accessed October 9, 2019

100. Patterson, Paige. *A Pilgrim Priesthood*, (Eugene, OR: Wipf & Stock Publishers, 2004), 165

101. Powers, Daniel G. *1 & 2 Peter, Jude: a Commentary in the Wesleyan Tradition*. (Kansas City, MO: Beacon Hill Press, 2010), 137

102. Roy S. Nicholson in *The Beacon Bible Commentary: Hebrews through Revelation, Vol. 10* (Kansas City, MO: Beacon Hill Press, 1967), 297

**Devotion 26**

103. Clifton Fadiman & André Bernard, General Editors, *Bartlett's Book of Anecdotes* (New York: Little Brown & Company,1985), 329

104. Paige Patterson, *A Pilgrim Priesthood* (Eugene, OR: Wipf & Stock Publishers, 2004), 168

105. D. Edmund Hiebert, *1 Peter* (Winona Lake, IL: BMH Books, 1992), 288

106. Charles S. Ball, *The Wesleyan Bible Commentary Vol. VI* (Grand Rapids, MI: Baker Book House, 1966), 271

107. Ben Witherington III, *Letters and Homilies for Hellenized Christians, Vol. II* (Downer's Grove, IL: Inter-Varsity Press, 2007), 216

108. Allen Satterlee, *Notable Quotables: a Compendium of Gems from Salvation Army Literature* (Atlanta: The Salvation Army, 1985), 90

109. William Barclay, *The Letters of James and Peter* (Philadelphia: The Westminster Press, 1960), 310

**Devotion 27**

110. Craig Brian Larson, *750 Engaging Illustrations for Preachers, Teachers and Writers* (Grand Rapids, MI: Baker Books), 151

111. D. Edmund Hiebert, *1 Peter* (Winona Lake, IL: BMH Books, 1992), 300

112 .Ben Witherington III, *Letters and Homilies for Hellenized Christians, Vol. II* (Downer's Grove, IL: Inter-Varsity Press, 2007), 227

113. Ibid., 228

114. Paige Patterson, *A Pilgrim Priesthood* (Eugene, OR: Wipf & Stock Publishers, 2004), 181

115. Ben Witherington III, *Letters and Homilies for Hellenized Christians, Vol. II* (Downer's Grove, IL: Inter-Varsity Press, 2007), 229

**Devotion 28**
116. Clifford Fadiman & André Bernard, *Bartlett's Book of Anecdotes* (New York: Little, Brown & Company, 1985), 98-99
117. William Barclay, *The Letters of James and Peter* (Philadelphia: The Westminster Press, 1960), 321
118. *Wesley Bible Studies* (Indianapolis, IN: Wesleyan Publishing House, 2014), 76
119. William Barclay, *The Letters of James and Peter* (Philadelphia: The Westminster Press, 1960), 321
120. Roy S. Nicholson, *Beacon Bible Commentary, Hebrews-Revelation Vol. 10* (Kansas City, MO: Beacon Hill Press, 1967), 301
121. D. Edmund Hiebert, *1 Peter* (Winona Lake, IL: BMH Books, 1992), 311

**Devotion 29**
122. Tony Evans, *Tony Evans Book of Illustrations* (Chicago: Moody Publishers, 2009), 166-167
123. D. Edmund Hiebert, *1 Peter* (Winona Lake, IL: BMH Books, 1992), 315
124. Allen Satterlee, *In the Balance: Christ Weighs the Heart of Seven Churches* (Alexandria, VA: Crest Books, 2013), 82-84
125. David A. Case & David W. Holdren, *1-2 Peter, 1-3 John, Jude: A Commentary for Bible Students* (Indianapolis, IN: Wesleyan Publishing House, 2005), 131